I'm Taking You Another Way

A Slightly Less Than Normal Life

By
Jeffery L. Stockford

I'm Taking You Another Way

Trilogy Christian Publishers

A Wholly Owned Subsidiary of Trinity Broadcasting Network

2442 Michelle Drive, Tustin, CA 92780

Copyright © 2024 by Jeffery L. Stockford

Scripture quotations marked AMP are taken from the Amplified® Bible (AMP), Copyright © 2015 by The Lockman Foundation. Used by permission. www.Lockman.org.

Scripture quotations marked MSG are taken from *THE MESSAGE,* copyright (c) 1993, 2002, 2018 by Eugene H. Peterson. Used by permission of NavPress. All rights reserved. Represented by Tyndale House Publishers, Inc.

Scripture quotations marked NIV are taken from the Holy Bible, New International Version®, NIV®. Copyright © 1973, 1978, 1984, 2011 by Biblica, Inc.™ Used by permission of Zondervan. All rights reserved worldwide. www.zondervan.com. The "NIV" and "New International Version" are trademarks registered in the United States Patent and Trademark Office by Biblica, Inc.™

Scripture quotations marked NKJV are taken from the New King James Version®. Copyright © 1982 by Thomas Nelson. Used by permission. All rights reserved.

Scripture quotations marked NLT are taken from the Holy Bible, New Living Translation, copyright © 1996, 2004, 2015 by Tyndale House Foundation. Used by permission of Tyndale House Publishers, Inc., Carol Stream, Illinois 60188. All rights reserved.

Scripture quotations marked TLV are taken from the Tree of Life (TLV) Translation of the Bible. Copyright © 2015 by The Messianic Jewish Family Bible Society.

All rights reserved, including the right to reproduce this book or portions thereof in any form whatsoever.

For information, address Trilogy Christian Publishing

Rights Department, 2442 Michelle Drive, Tustin, CA 92780.

Trilogy Christian Publishing/ TBN and colophon are trademarks of Trinity Broadcasting Network.

For information about special discounts for bulk purchases, please contact Trilogy Christian Publishing.

Trilogy Disclaimer: The views and content expressed in this book are those of the author and may not necessarily reflect the views and doctrine of Trilogy Christian Publishing or the Trinity Broadcasting Network.

10 9 8 7 6 5 4 3 2 1

Library of Congress Cataloging-in-Publication Data is available.

ISBN 979-9-89041-959-0

ISBN (ebook) 979-9-89041-960-6

Endorsements

Beautiful melodies and inspiring lyrics, combined with a passionate heart for Christ and dedicated ministry for His glory, mark the wonderful testimony of Jeff Stockford!

Scott Wesley Brown, *Singer/Songwriter, Veteran CCM Artist, Minister*

Jeff has used his amazing talent as a gifted songwriter and accomplished musician. His ability to capture an audience is both entertaining and divine. Even this title, *I'm Taking You Another Way*, speaks of Jeff's creativity and thinking outside the box. Get ready to journey down a road of inspiration as you read this genuine work.

Pasco A. Manzo, President/CEO Adult & Teen Challenge New England and New Jersey

Jeff Stockford is "that person" you meet and stay friends with for life. It doesn't matter if you talk with him every ten minutes or every ten years, the covenant love from his relationship with Jesus keeps it fresh. His gentle but laser focused demeanor as a communicator, be it spoken or sung, will weave grace into your heart. On a side note, if you love guitars, you're in his tight circle.

Paul Clark, *Singer/Songwriter, Producer, CCM Pioneer, Minister*

Jeff Stockford cannot be easily described, but if I had to do it in one sentence it would be: A multifaceted, complex, simple man. He is amazingly intelligent, exceptionally talented, and extraordinarily gifted. But those tremendous attributes are all delicately and discreetly housed behind the most Christlike and touching humility I have ever seen in anyone. Jeff was my pastor and is my friend. As I read this book, I laughed and cried and thought about what a blessing Jeff is to me.

Tom Hardin, *President and Founder, National Association of Safety Professionals, Bible Teacher*

Foreword

I am writing the foreword that my father, Charles H. Cookman, would be writing had he lived to see the publication of Jeff's story. I cannot do this project justice. For now, just know that Dad is cheering this story along with a hearty "*Think of that!*" and I am basking in an ocean of invigorating sentiment.

I am glad I did not have to live these past 45-plus years without Jeff Stockford in my life. That is, without Jeff and the world around him which he has enriched with his person, personality, music, words, humor, sincerity, and most of all, the transcendent presence of Another living in and through him. There really is "Another" (*An Other*) who superintends "another (*an other*) way." And, for those who know him personally, Jeff has made it functionally impossible to disbelieve this.

There is no doubt that Jeff is intellectually astute, yet without the acidity that too often accompanies a sharp mind and quick wit. He's as humble as the most curious of students. My family and friends have, so often, enjoyed his talents – music, poetry, drama, humor, and poignant messages that held me spell-bound. He is constantly saying things that I wish I had said. He's brilliant.

But none of that is what one first notices about Jeff. No, this big ball of wonder comes to us as unintimidating as a baby in a make-shift crib. And hopefully, this story will come to you in that same spirit. If you let it, it will at once be instructive, insightful, therapeutic, delightful, and truly inspirational.

In a sense, you will not read this biography, you will absorb it. I do not merely read Jeff's artful writings or listen to his amazing music – I absorb him. I sense him. I am affected by him.

Whatever encouragement you get from this book, I hope that what my father saw *and felt* coming from within Jeff is imparted to you. It is the tenderness of heart and mind that comes from another world, fleshed out in a man who is willing to be led "another way." It comes in the spirit of Him who *is* that other world.

Many years ago, I was deeply affected by a short scene when my dad and Jeff connected. Jeff had made a long drive to do a concert for a "youth camp" held for preacher's kids, something my dad did each year for the kids of all the preachers in his care. Jeff was tired and went to his room in the cabin where my dad and I also had a room. He needed a quick nap before the night's concert. My dad saw Jeff resting, quietly went to his bedside where Jeff was sleeping, knelt down, placed his hands on Jeff, and began to pray for him. Dad knew some of Jeff's story and shared some of the same sense of difficulties going back to childhood. Dad was always compassionate and felt strongly for people who were hurting or struggling. I could see the fatherly tenderness in that moment, and it drew me in.

But that's not the scene that most affected me. Later, Jeff told me of the moment. He was not asleep. He heard everything my father had prayed and had felt the warmth of his touch, a reassuring warmth that I had experienced so often and miss so much to this day. It was as funny as it was touching. Jeff remained perfectly still – almost frozen - concerned that if he moved (if only to acknowledge Dad's presence), he would somehow interfere with and stop the moment. To Jeff (and to me) it was a sacred moment on hallowed ground that was part of *another way*.

Yes. I'm glad I have Jeff and his family in my life. And now, I am overjoyed to have his story in print, a soul-script simmering in my psyche where it nourishes and enriches me...always.

Noel H. Cookman

Table of Contents

Endorsements	5
Foreword	7
Preface	11
Chapter 1 - A ROUGH START	13
Chapter 2 - SUNSHINE STATE	17
Chapter 3 - FIRST DATE (WITH AN OLDER WOMAN)	21
Chapter 4 - BOMB FOUND AT DISNEY	25
Chapter 5 - A LONELY EXISTENCE	29
Chapter 6 - FLYING FISTS	33
Chapter 7 - ONE MAN'S TRASH IS ANOTHER MAN'S TREASURE	39
Chapter 8 - THE GOOD NEWS CLUB	43
Chapter 9 - A SPIRITUAL FATHER	49
Chapter 10 - THE MAKING OF A PSALMIST	55
Chapter 11 - MAN MAKERS	59
Chapter 12 - FLEW THE COOP	63
Chapter 13 - MY WORLD JUST GOT BIGGER	67
Chapter 14 - A PAINFUL LESSON	71
Chapter 15 - MY LITTLE BUDDY	75
Chapter 16 - I DIDN'T SEE THAT COMING	79
Chapter 17 - THE LOVE OF MY LIFE	85
Chapter 18 - DRINKING POISON	91
Chapter 19 - THE POWERFUL ANTIDOTE	95
Chapter 20 – LATE NIGHT BUFFETS	97

Chapter 21 - THUMP-THUMP, THUMP-THUMP	101
Chapter 22 - Uncharted Waters	105
Chapter 23 - Hard Decisions	111
Chapter 24 - Church Planting is Not for the Faint of Heart	119
Chapter 25 - A Genuine Shepherd and a Lifelong Friend	125
Chapter 26 - Yenz Aren't from Around Here	129
Chapter 27 - A Game Changer	133
Chapter 28 - A Strange Assignment	137
Chapter 29 - The Man with a Kind Voice	141
Chapter 30 - "My Masterpiece"	147
Chapter 31 - Help! I Think My Mom Married an Assassin!	153
Chapter 32 - Training Unaware	157
Chapter 33 - Crime Scene	159
Chapter 34 - What's a Guy Like Me Doing in a Place Like This?	163
Chapter 35 - The Vote	167
Chapter 36 - Hand Frozen to the Sword	175
Chapter 37 - A Blunt and Bent Nail	183
Chapter 38 - A Place I Never Imagined	189

Preface

Back when I was in my mid-40's, I had a most unusual dream... In the dream I arrived in a group of tour buses in the mall area of Washington D.C.. The passengers were getting off the buses and congregating around their assigned tour guides who were holding various colored flags. I was the last person off the bus, and upon stepping down, I started looking to see where my particular group was gathering. I spotted them over to my left and began to move in their direction. After one step, I looked over to my right and saw Jesus standing there alone. He looked at me, smiled, and motioned with His hand for me to come to Him. I looked over at the group I was supposed to be with, as they were preparing to leave. Instead of going to them I walked toward Jesus, but started to explain to Him that I was supposed to be with that group. Jesus put His hand on my shoulder and said, *"No, son, I'm taking you another way."* I agreed to go with Him, forgetting about the group and somehow knowing that this tour would be unlike anything the others were going to experience.

I awoke and this was one of the few dreams in my life that I can remember. I believe Jesus' words in my dream, *"I'm taking you another way,"* have characterized my entire life. His route has taken me on a very circuitous journey. It has not always been easy or comfortable, and at times it seemed impossible. But I am so glad I decided to follow Him.

This book is a collection of stories, events, life lessons, and a stockpile of experiences my Heavenly Tour Guide led me through. He has used these to shape me and set my course.

I write this book to the glory of my Lord and Savior, Jesus Christ. He is the true and only hero of my story! I want my life to (as my friend David Hughes says) "brag on Jesus!"

The things I've written about are from my (admittedly limited) perspective. Some persons referenced in this book may hold a different view. As the late Queen Elizabeth famously said, "Recollections may vary." I've also changed some of the names of different individuals to protect their privacy.

Another reason for writing this is to leave an account of the journey I've traveled for my dearly loved and precious granddaughter, Solveig Shoshana. Perhaps one day she will benefit and gain some wisdom from this book that will help her on her own journey as she fulfills her destiny in God.

I dedicate this book to her.

Chapter 1

A Rough Start

The details concerning my birth and early childhood are sketchy at best. But here's what I know... I was born on October 11, 1961, in Pontiac, Michigan, to my parents, James Herald and Geraldine Crane Stockford. I had two other older siblings at the time, Kalvin and Terri.

My mother was from Central Florida and I'm not sure how she wound up in Pontiac, Michigan, but that is where she met and married my father. I have absolutely no information on how they met. They never spoke about it in our family as far as I know.

Later in life, my mother told me a story that I can't verify. But I believed it because I had nothing else to counter her account, plus you want to believe your own mother, right?

She said that when she found out she was pregnant with me, she told my father. He wasn't very happy to hear that there was going to be another mouth to feed and got pretty upset. Later in the pregnancy she caught a bad cold and needed some medicine from the drug store. She claimed that my father was friends with the pharmacist and that he asked the pharmacist for some pills that would cause her to have a miscarriage.

After she took the pills, she found out what he had done. I don't know if he confessed or how she found out. She was not a Christian and didn't have any religious background, but she said that she prayed and asked God to spare me. God answered her prayer (obviously).

The next event took place about a month before I was born. This is something my father relayed to me at some point. He told me that my mother was extremely allergic to poison ivy and had somehow come into contact with it. She had a severe reaction to it, and he described her as, "swelling up like a beach ball." This endangered not only her life but also the baby (me). Once again, she prayed that God would spare her baby's life. She was given a procedure to prolong her pregnancy and prevent her from going into labor. As it turns out, she was able to give birth safely, and TA-DA, here I am!

They brought me home from the hospital to a small apartment that was above a garage. A few weeks later, my mother was getting ready to take me to the doctor for a routine post-delivery checkup. It was already chilly in Michigan, so she left me momentarily in the care of my 3-year-old brother and 2-year-old sister, while she went downstairs into the garage to warm up the car.

She turned on the ignition, started the heater, and as she stepped out of the car, she saw a horrifying sight. My brother, Kalvin, had picked me up and brought me to the edge of the concrete steps, and said, "Mama, you forgot your baby." Then I slipped from his arms and proceeded to roll down the entire flight of stairs (thanks, bro!). Apparently, there were no injuries to my 3-week-old body. I'm not sure I can say the same for my big brother's backside after pulling a stunt like that. Despite not having any visible injuries, some who have heard this story tend to think that I was probably dropped on my head.

One day, decades later, my mother told me that after these events, and seeing how God answered her prayers for my protection, she determined early on that He had some special purpose for my life.

14   I'm Taking You Another Way

When she told me this, I thought of the Bible verse, Luke 2:19 NKJV. At the birth of Jesus, the shepherds came to visit the little family in the stable. They spoke to Mary and Joseph of what the angel had told them. Then it says in verse 19... "But Mary kept all these things and pondered them in her heart."

Before I formed you in the womb I knew you; Before you were born I sanctified you; I ordained you a prophet to the nations.

Jeremiah 1:5 NKJV

Chapter 2

Sunshine State

This story was relayed to me by my father. On a cold Michigan day, when I was about six weeks old, my father took my mother and me to an outdoor strip mall near our home. He dropped us off on one end of the mall with instructions that he would pick us up at the same place (or so he thought) in about an hour. He came back after an hour and waited for a long amount of time, but my mom and I were nowhere in sight.

After about 45 minutes, he started driving the length of the strip mall trying to find us. He finally spotted us at the extreme opposite end of the strip mall standing on the sidewalk, wet and shivering. Apparently, there was a miscommunication and/or misunderstanding. He collected his cold, wet, angry wife and infant son, and as one might imagine, a big argument ensued. He later told me that my mother was convinced that he had done that on purpose.

Whether this was an isolated incident or an accumulation of similar offenses, I do not know. However, the next day while my father was at work, she loaded up her clothes, personal belongings, and her three small children in a car and began driving, leaving Michigan and heading to Orlando, Florida, the Sunshine State.

She had some family in Florida, namely her aunt, Beth Whidden. Aunt Beth was a never-married single woman with her own house. She was what was referred to at that time as a "private nurse." She would provide nursing care in people's homes, mostly the wealthy. In fact, one of her most notable patients was Thomas Alva Edison, when he broke his hip in 1930.

I don't know what kind of relationship Aunt Beth had with my mother, but she welcomed my mother and us kids into her home permanently. My mother told me that when she got to the front door of the house, she placed me in Aunt Beth's arms and then collapsed from sheer exhaustion from the long drive. There at 37 East Rosevear Street, we lived as a family until I was 17 years old and moved out. I don't know how long after our arrival that my father arrived at the house in Orlando. But at some point, perhaps a few months later, he was reconciled to my mother and joined us.

I am amazed at the extreme generosity of my Great Aunt Beth, to take in her niece's family. She basically helped raise, feed, and clothe a family with three small children. At the time my young mind thought this was all normal. I didn't have anything to compare it to. She babysat us during the day, and then worked each night in her nursing job.

As part of the arrangement for us living there, my father provided transportation for her, to and from her various work assignments. Aunt Beth's eyesight was beginning to fail, and she wasn't able to drive. I have many fond memories of riding in the backseat with my father to go pick her up around 7:00 a.m. most mornings. I've always been an early riser.

I liked listening to the country music radio station my father would play and strangely found the smell of his cigarettes sort of comforting. It was something that became a routine. I don't remember any conversations, only a quiet ride in the dark, with the music of Ray Price, Bobby Goldsboro, Skeeter Davis, Johnny Cash,

Lynn Anderson, Porter Wagoner and others, softly playing. This is probably where I began to develop my love for music.

Though I have lived in many places, I will always remember Orlando, Florida fondly. It is where I grew up, went to school, and most importantly, where I met my Lord and Savior, Jesus Christ.

Whenever I go back to visit my old neighborhood, it always strikes me how small the houses and yards are. When I was a kid, it was my whole universe.

He who calls you is faithful, who also will do it.

1 Thessalonians 5:24 NKJV

Chapter 3

First Date
(With an Older Woman)

My time in elementary school wasn't anything remarkable. I only have some fragmented memories here and there. I do, however, remember crying often (which also embarrassed me). I was a very tender-hearted child and even when I got angry I started crying, which resulted in the other kids calling me a crybaby... which made me angry, which made me cry. As you can see, it was a vicious cycle. In my early elementary school years, I had mostly older, grandmotherly ladies as my teachers, but when I reached the fifth grade, that changed!

I showed up to Princeton Elementary School, a ten-year-old, awkward, shy boy. It was there I met my new teacher, Miss H. She was 27 years old and was absolutely beautiful. I didn't know there were any beautiful young teachers out there! I remember staring at her, as did most of the little boys in our class. I wanted to make her like me and do everything she wanted and more.

I went home and told my mom and Aunt Beth about my wonderful new teacher. For the first time I didn't dread going to school. I also made my first friend. He was a blind boy named David. Miss H asked for a volunteer to help escort David around the school, letting him hold onto their arm. I gladly offered myself and we became buddies that year.

A few months into the school year, a big event occurred in Orlando... the opening of Walt Disney World. Everyone was extremely excited. I heard some of the other children in our class talk about their experience and I wished that I could go too. When I asked my mother about going, she said, "Why don't you ask your pretty teacher if you can 'escort' her to Walt Disney World?" I don't know if she really meant it, but I acted upon her suggestion.

The next day at school, at the end of the water fountain line, I found myself standing alone beside Miss H. I swallowed hard, took a deep breath, and said, "My mom said I should ask you if I can escort you to Disney World some time." I wasn't even sure what escort meant. She smiled and said, "Yes, I think that would be nice. I'll let you know when we can go." I think I must have floated all the way home that day.

About two weeks later came the day. My mom sent me to school in a black suit and a yellow tie. Of course I stood out like a sore thumb, but I didn't care! I was going to Disney World with my beautiful teacher!

After school, we got in her yellow Volkswagen Beetle and went to her house. I remember sitting quietly in her living room drinking a glass of water. She came out of her bedroom, and we got in the car.

The first time going to Walt Disney World was overwhelming to me. There was so much to take in, I was probably on sensory overload. The few things I can remember was us eating lunch, going into The Country Bear Jamboree, The Jungle Cruise, A Small World, and The Haunted Mansion. She must have sensed that I was scared on The Haunted Mansion ride and reached down and tapped my hand. I recall thinking, *She is so wonderful, and I think she must really like me.* Trust me, it was nothing remotely sexual in any way; that part of my brain was not developed at that point. I believe God, in His foresight and love, brought her into my life that year, in preparation for what was about to occur in about three or four months.

I will always be thankful for Miss H. After I became an adult and recorded my first album, I traveled back to Orlando to sing at a church. I looked her up and found that she was still teaching at Princeton Elementary. I met her after school to tell her what she meant to my life, and to thank her for going above and beyond her job description to help a broken, love-starved little boy. I gave her a signed copy of my album, "Late Night Buffets." I never saw or heard from her again after that, but I am grateful to have had the chance to see her one more time.

Finally, all of you be of one mind, having compassion for one another; love as brothers, be tenderhearted, be courteous;

1 Peter 3:8 NKJV

Chapter 4

Bomb Found at Disney

One night in early February of 1972, something bizarre took place in our home. Us kids had already gone to bed, but a little later my mother woke us up and called us out into the living room. She showed us a newspaper, the *Orlando Sentinel Star*, with a shocking headline. The headline said, "BOMB FOUND AT DISNEY!" Beneath the headline was a photo of my father in handcuffs, being taken into custody. For some unknown reason, he was smiling in the photo.

At that moment we were all in shock. I do not remember anything being explained, or even any questions being asked. We were shown the newspaper and then sent back to bed. I guess back in those days, that generation of parents didn't explain a lot to their kids. At least that is what I've observed.

What I have put together from the little information I have is that my father had gotten into some financial trouble and made bomb threats to Walt Disney World, Dr. P. Phillips Citrus Plant, and Ivey's Department Store (now Dillard's), in order to extort one million dollars. An explosive device was found in a maintenance shed somewhere in the Magic Kingdom. As far as the other places, I've never heard of any bombs found there. I was told by someone that the extortion letters were hand-written with calligraphy in Old English style. Incidentally, my father was a gifted artist and could draw with a pencil and it would look almost like a black and white photograph. He could have easily written those notes.

Two weeks prior to him being arrested, he left our family. No explanation was ever given to me. Within those two weeks, he drove by the park in our neighborhood. My brother Kalvin and I were playing there, and when my brother spotted my dad's car, we both ran to see him. At one point he asked if we wanted to see something, he then opened the trunk and showed us a bunch of guns. I got scared and ran home.

Another incident occurred during those two weeks leading up to my father's arrest which is somehow related; however, I don't know exactly how... I was in my mother's bedroom, which also had its own front door entrance. A man came to the door wearing sunglasses. He knocked on the door and I ran to answer. I opened it and he asked, "Is your father here?" Before I could get a word out, my mother flew across the room, jerked my arm, pulled me back, and slammed and locked the door in his face. She started yelling, "He's not here, he's not here!" The man left after that.

She then turned to me and slapped my face so hard it sent me flying back onto the bed. I started crying and asked, "What did I do?" She then started cussing and saying, "Didn't you see he had a gun in his hand?"

I can only speculate that this guy was some kind of debt collector or hitman, coming to settle something with my father. I heard some time later that my father's work truck was found abandoned and riddled with bullet holes. He must have made some bad people very angry.

Again, no explanation as to what was going on or why my mother reacted so strongly. It was not uncommon for my parents and Aunt

Beth to use violence on us kids, beyond a normal spanking. During the course of my childhood, I had teeth knocked out, a black eye, and bleeding stripes on my back. In my world that was normal; however, the hard face slapping that occurred when this mystery man came to our door will always stand out in my mind as especially harsh and unjustified.

My father was convicted and sentenced to prison at Raeford State Penitentiary, where I believe he served about three-and-a-half-years of his sentence and was then placed in a work release program. He would be released to paint a historic hotel in Orlando, then go back to prison at night.

My mother filed for divorce from my father after he was convicted. The day the divorce was final, my mother walked up to me playing in the back yard and said, "This has been all your fault." I don't know why she said that, but I believed her, and carried a sense of guilt around for years.

Although a bomb never went off at the places my father threatened, he effectively detonated our family. I will have more about my father later in this book.

The Lord is merciful and gracious,
slow to anger, and abounding in mercy.

Psalm 103:8 NKJV

Chapter 5

A Lonely Existence

As a child, I never had a problem with being by myself. My siblings were either older or too young to be playmates (my parents had adopted two baby girls when I was in the second and third grade). I was content playing by myself most of the time. I had some G.I. Joe and Johnny West (cowboy) action figures. My most prized possession and my favorite Christmas gift as a child was a set of Bonanza action figures: Ben, Hoss, and Little Joe. So, playing alone, creating scenarios for my action figures, kept me entertained. I also learned to ride a two-wheeler bicycle around this time and began to venture out into my neighborhood, riding up and down the street and around the block. I think at this point in time is when I realized how alone I felt.

There were a few houses on my street that had some boys close to my age. However, some of them picked on and bullied me in school, so I didn't really want to hang around them. These boys did normal things like ride BMX dirt bikes and stuff like that. I was that wimpy kid who lived with that strange family, three houses down.

School was a mixed bag for me. I was often the recipient of ridicule and rejection. Our class would be coming in from recess and some kid would say, "Last one in their seat loves Jeff Stockford!" And a race would then ensue. But at the same time, I had my blind friend, David, to escort, and there was my kind teacher, Miss H. She knew of my situation at home, as did most of my class, and I think she showed me a little more attention and felt compassion for me. My sense of isolation and loneliness only grew from that point. I longed for a true friend and to be loved.

My mother began to date a few men, and eventually she would bring them over to meet her five children. I remember two of them especially. One was a man named Andy and he owned a gas station in College Park near our house. I remember him being big and very strong. He was also a happy, kind, and gentle man. I had hoped he and my mom would get married, but their relationship didn't last very long.

Another man she dated was also named Andy. He owned a local laundromat and was much older than my mother. He was also kind and supplied us with various flavors of generic canned sodas. That relationship didn't make it very long either, but it was nice while it lasted.

She put an ad in the personal section of the newspaper to find a husband, and got a response from a man in Stuart, Florida, named Carl Otis Walker. Stuart is a coastal town two hours south of Orlando. He drove up to meet her and us kids. He was a widower and had a nine-year-old daughter named Betty Sue.

They met, and after only three days, decided to get married. I remember my mom coming down the hallway to each of our bedrooms to tell us they were getting married. It was in the evening and we were getting ready for bed. After they came to my bedroom to give me the news, they said, "Goodnight," and Carl kissed me on my head. That kind gesture made me feel wonderful. My own father had never once expressed any affection for me that I can recall.

Betty Sue, my new stepsister, became my pal, and I took her under my wing to teach her the ropes. We were pretty close in age, and we spent a lot of time together. My mother was a beautician and had her own rented beauty shop. Carl was an auto body mechanic and procured a garage to do body work, two doors down from the beauty shop. They rode in to work together and came home together every evening. They ate most of their meals out, so we kids had to fend for ourselves. They provided ample amounts of groceries but left it up to us or Aunt Beth to prepare most of the time.

This newly combined family didn't remain peaceful very long. The trouble at 37 East Rosevear Street was just getting started.

Turn to me and be gracious to me,
for I am lonely and afflicted.

Psalm 25:16 NIV

Chapter 6

Flying Fists

My brother Kalvin had difficulty accepting Carl as his stepfather. I think he felt as if he were being disloyal to our real father. There always seemed to be tension between them, and one day it boiled over. I don't know what started it because I was in my bedroom, but Kalvin must have hit Carl. I heard the yelling and cussing from the other room. I stuck my head out of the door and heard Carl ask, "You gonna hit me again?!" Then I saw him punch Kalvin in the face, knocking him back onto the bed. Kalvin shouted, "Next time it will be with a (expletive) brick!"

Kalvin was probably about 14 and was a big boy, and Carl was a small man. However, Carl was a former volunteer fireman/police officer in Stuart, Florida, so he knew how to handle himself. He was a rough and tough man originally from Beckley, West Virginia. You've heard the saying that dynamite comes in small packages? Well, that certainly applied to Carl.

Kalvin left our house and I assume he stayed with one of his friends. Over the course of the previous tumultuous year, he had gotten in with a bad group of boys in our area. He had started smoking and eventually that led to him taking drugs.

He ended up at a juvenile prison farm for boys. He would be there for six months, be released, and then commit some other act that would get him locked up again. This cycle was repeated over and over until he was an adult.

I wanted to get along with my new stepfather. I tried to be respectful, for the most part. The fact that I refused to side with Kalvin against Carl made Kalvin hate me. During the rest of my time in that house, I only saw him a few times after the big fight with Carl.

My older sister Terri was kind of quiet and stayed in the background. I don't remember having a lot of interaction with her back then, but I know she was always looking out for me. She spent most of her time helping care for our two adopted little sisters. She eventually married someone, but the marriage ended in divorce a few years later after she found notes from other women in his car. She was a professional beautician and worked in my mom's beauty parlor for several years. Terri is about the sweetest person I've ever known. I can't remember a single time she was mean to me growing up. I love her very much!

Sixth grade was a not-so-good year for me as well. I had a different teacher who didn't take the same kind of interest in me as Miss H had. She wasn't mean or anything like that, but I felt as if I had lost my only ally. There were a few disciplinary actions taken against me, which were well deserved. They were most likely due to me smarting off to her when I got angry, and I was angry a lot!

One day in the library, some of the kids were talking about this exciting new TV show, called *Star Trek*. We started to talk about Mr. Spock and how he had this Vulcan technique, where he could squeeze your shoulder and render you unconscious. The group was debating on whether it was something real. Wanting to gain some respect without thinking it through, I chimed in, "I know how to do the Vulcan Shoulder Squeeze."

For a moment they were in awe of me. I suddenly became "bad-to-the-bone." I finally had the respect that I'd craved for so long (it only lasted about ten seconds). One of the boys named John, a kid with a five-o'clock-shadow and a full mustache in the sixth grade, spoke up and said, "Oh yeah, why don't you show me that after school, Stockford?" My heart sunk down to my shoes. This was a kid that nobody messed with. I swallowed hard and replied, "Okay."

The best strategy I could come up with was to get to my bike as fast as I could when the bell rang. Then maybe I could get far enough away before he could find me. Maybe by Monday he would have forgotten about it.

There was a vacant lot about a block away from the school. It was where all the school fights took place. There was no way to avoid it on my route home. Time was of the essence!

The bell rang. I made a beeline to the bike rack, got on my Schwinn, and put the pedal to the metal. As I approached the vacant lot, I noticed a crowd had already formed. Were they let out of class early to witness the event? Sure enough, there was John waiting for me to demonstrate my Vulcan skills. I'd never tried it, but I was pretty sure the ol' shoulder squeeze thing was not going to achieve the desired result, so my mind started racing for an alternative. I thought, when I approach him instead of reaching for his shoulder, I'll give him a side kick in the stomach, and then run like the wind before he can catch me. By the way, I'm like the old Howlin' Wolf blues song, "I'm built for comfort, I ain't built for speed..."

Well, as soon as I raised my leg to kick him (Chuck Norris I'm not), he blocked it and the only thing I remember was a large hairy fist coming toward my face at a high velocity. I felt a thud and I hit the ground, knocked out cold. Everyone must have scattered and a couple of the boys on my street helped me onto my bike and held my handlebars to get me home. I had a black eye for about a month after that.

The next fight I got in was toward the end of that school year. A boy named Karl decided he wanted to beat me up after school. He was a bully in our school (at least towards me).

Once again, I tried to make a hasty retreat and get home before he could find me. I rode past the vacant lot without seeing anyone waiting for me. I sighed with relief and rode the next half mile or so in relative peace. But when I rounded the corner of my street, I saw a group of about six boys on their bikes blocking the street about one hundred feet from my driveway. They had set a roadblock and there was no running away.

The boys surrounded me and started egging Karl on to fight me (not that he needed any encouragement). I had a reputation of being a wimp because of the last incident, and because of my quiet, non-tough demeanor. It was fun for them to have someone to pick on and I was a great candidate.

As I was surrounded, Karl took off his belt and started snapping it at me like a whip. One of the times I was able to grab it and jerk it from his hands. Then he went to give me a karate kick to the face. Miraculously, I was able to grab his foot which made him lose his balance and fall to the ground. Something inside said, "It's now or never!" So, I jumped on him and started hitting him with my fists as hard as I could. Then I grabbed a handful of his hair and started smashing his head against the curb. He started crying and saying, "I give up! I give up!" I let him up while the other boys stood there with their mouths open.

I don't know what happened that day, but something snapped. I don't know what would have happened if it wasn't stopped. He stood up, crying and red in the face. He said that he was going to bring a pocketknife to school the next day and kill me. Then he left to go to his house.

I looked up and saw my mom standing at the end of the driveway. I was expecting to be in trouble, but as it turned out, she was proud of me. She fixed me an after-school snack and sat down with me while I was eating. I wasn't used to this kind of treatment, but I liked it!

While eating, I looked out the window and saw a woman with a bouffant hairstyle and Karl coming up to my front door. The woman was Karl's mother. She had buzzed his hair into a crew-cut, which is what happened back in those days when parents weaponized haircuts as a punishment. She made him apologize and said, "He does not even own a pocketknife and he is not going to bother you anymore." Wow! I didn't see that coming!

The next day I saw Karl at school. He came up to me and asked if it would be okay if he told everyone our fight was a tie. I don't know why I agreed to his request, but I did. He then took a swing at me when I wasn't looking and I turned around and punched him in the stomach, right in plain view of the school principal. We were both suspended for three days. I don't remember having any more trouble with him after that.

O Lord, keep me out of the hands of the wicked. Protect me from those who are violent, for they are plotting against me.

Psalm 140:4 NLT

Chapter 7

One Man's Trash is Another Man's Treasure

For the kids in our neighborhood, a lot of excitement was centered around the local 7-Eleven convenience store. Every two weeks the flavor of Slurpee changed, and we waited with great anticipation to see and taste it. Any new product or flavor of...candy, potato chips, soda, etc. generated quite a buzz on the street! Most of us would spend our allowance on candy and potato chips (my personal favorite was BBQ).

Next door to the 7-Eleven was an antique store which held very little interest to me. I was already surrounded by old junky stuff at home. Why would I want to look at someone else's old junky stuff? But one day I decided to go in there out of sheer boredom. I noticed a sign in the front that said, "WE BUY ANTIQUES." I asked the owner how that worked, and he informed me that I could bring in an antique and he would assess its value and give me cash on the spot.

I excitedly went home and began searching for a qualifying object I could sell. Out in our utility shed, there was a rusty old iron that had been there as long as I could remember. It was the old-timey kind that wasn't electric but had to be heated on a stove or hot coals. It was used as a door stop and had been painted over several times with flakes of paint chipping off.

I thought that nobody would miss it and I could get some serious cash for this worthless piece of junk. I took it up to the antique store and the man there determined its value to be a whopping $2. That WAS some serious cash for a kid like me! The transaction was made and with those two bucks burning a hole in my pocket, I headed next door to the 7-Eleven and bought everything my heart desired and more. I felt like a king!

I couldn't take any of it home because I wasn't inclined to share with any of my siblings. So, I went to a bench outside a Presbyterian church near my house and consumed all of my treasures with great satisfaction.

I don't know how much time elapsed, maybe a few weeks, but what I had done was discovered. My mother and my stepfather, Carl, came in my bedroom and wanted to know what happened to the old antique iron from the utility shed.

Me, not thinking I had done anything wrong, calmly said that I had sold it to the antique store guy for $2. My mother started crying and when I asked why, Carl reared back and hit me in the face with his fist, giving me another black eye. My mother said that item was the only thing she had left that belonged to her father. I don't remember what happened after that, except that I stayed in my room and didn't eat any supper. I couldn't help reasoning in my brain that it must not have been all that sentimental if you painted over it and used it as a doorstop in a dirty utility shed.

The next day at school, my P.E. teacher, Coach Tony, asked me about the big bruise on the side of my face and seemed genuinely concerned. I'd only recently learned of something called "child abuse," and that parents could get in trouble for it. He seemed as if he was ready to take some kind of action if I only gave him cause.

Sensing that if I told him how it happened, he might call the police, I thought I'd better keep it to myself or I'd really get in hot water. If Carl was arrested, our family would be in deep financial trouble and my mother would never forgive me. I felt like she already blamed me for the breakup of her marriage to my father. So, I made up some lame lie about walking into a pole or something. I don't think he was convinced and seemed disappointed that I wouldn't give him the real story. He looked me in the eye and asked if I was sure about it. He didn't press the matter any further, other than he assured me that if I wanted to talk about it, or anything, he would be available to listen. That act of concern warmed my heart, knowing that this man had me on his radar, and cared.

You might be wondering why I included the last two chapters, seeing as how there isn't really any spiritual content. Why even include these stories of violence? Believe me, there is much more I could write about that involved acts of physical abuse by my parents. There was also an incident of sexual abuse perpetrated by my brother, probably something he experienced himself in the juvenile detention center.

These are major events in my memory that have somehow shaped me and the course of my life, that eventually led me to my wonderful Savior, Jesus Christ. I do not write any of these things to make anyone feel sorry for me. I want you, dear reader, to see how deep the pit was, that Jesus, in His love, reached down to lift me out of.

A bruised reed He will not break, and smoking flax He will not quench, till He sends forth justice to victory;

Matthew 12:20 NKJV

Chapter 8

The Good News Club

Fast forward a few years to September of 1974. By this time, I was twelve years old and in the eighth grade at Robert E. Lee Junior High School. My situation had not improved. I lived in a tense and hostile environment. For most people, home is an oasis from the trouble and the negativity of the world. For me it was the opposite. My brother Kalvin had recently been arrested and sent to prison for physically assaulting a female police officer. My mom and stepfather mostly kept to themselves. My Great Aunt Beth was retired and was our babysitter.

When I came home from school, I'd unload my books and go hang out at Matthews Park, around the corner from my house. I'd walk around or sit on a bench until it started getting dark. Then I'd walk home, heat up a frozen pizza, take it back to my room to eat it, watch TV, then go to bed. That was my routine for a while.

One afternoon, I took a softball and a bat, and went to the park. I threw the ball in the air, hit it, then went to where it landed and hit it back. At least it was something to do to pass the time. Suddenly two young boys approached me and asked if they could chase the ball for me. I said, "Sure!" They seemed to enjoy playing fetch (which was essentially what it was). We took a break and sat down. Their names were Jimmy and Danny, eight and nine-year-old brothers who lived about a block and a half from the park. I enjoyed having someone to talk to, even though they were quite a bit younger than me.

The next day they did the same thing, and again the next. On Monday they asked me if I'd like to go with them to the Good News Club after school. They said they got to hear stories, sing songs, play games, and there were refreshments. The other stuff didn't really interest me, but I've always been fond of refreshments, so I agreed to go.

The next day, I met them at the park, and we rode our bikes to a little aqua colored cinderblock house. We entered to see a small group of young kids between the ages of six and nine. We were greeted by an elderly lady in a navy blouse and white skirt with a dark red wig. She had a British accent. Her name was Claire King, and she was a live-in nurse/assistant for the homeowner. She welcomed me with a warm smile and wrote down my name. I sat with the other kids on the sofa, dwarfing them, as I was already six feet two inches tall by that time.

Soon an older lady on crutches slowly entered the room from the back bedroom. My first impression was shock. At twelve, I had never seen someone so deformed. Her name was Ruth Bateson. She had been a missionary to Brazil for most of her adult life. She had never been married and had given herself completely to serving the Lord.

At some point she had developed a severe case of rheumatoid arthritis, which twisted her fingers and made her legs stiff. This was probably unrelated, but her appearance was like she had no chin. I couldn't help but stare at her most of the lesson.

She greeted the children and proceeded to lead the little meeting with songs from a cassette tape, while Ms. King held up boards with the lyrics on them. Then she told a Bible story, while another lady moved characters on a flannel board. After that, she took us through something called "The Wordless Book." It was a little booklet with only colored pages of black, red, white, gold and green. It went something like this:

"My heart was dark with sin until the Savior came in (black)
His precious blood I know (red)
Has washed me white as snow (white)
And then one day, I know I'll walk the streets of gold (gold)
To grow in Christ each day, I read my Bible and pray (green)"

(Author Unknown)

They gave me a little wordless book for my own. I wish I would have kept it.

While enjoying the much-anticipated refreshments (cookies and Kool-Aid), Ms. Bateson asked me if I was a Christian. I answered, "Yes." Then she asked me if I had ever asked Jesus to come into my heart to be my Savior. I said, "No." She then asked, "Do you want to go to heaven when you die and spend eternity with Jesus?" I answered, "I sure do!"

Ms. Bateson then led me in the "Sinner's Prayer." I repeated the words after her, but being self-conscious, I was also looking around to see who was watching me. After that I said goodbye, got on my big red Schwinn bike with a huge basket on the front (I called it my truck) and headed home. As soon as I got to my bedroom, I locked the door, knelt down, and prayed that prayer again as best as I could remember it, saying:

"Dear Jesus,

I know that I am a sinner.

I believe You died on the cross for me.

I ask You to come into my heart and be my Savior.

I love You!

Amen."

I stood up and declared out loud, "I'm going to be a preacher when I grow up!" From that point until this very day, I've never wanted to do anything else.

I returned to the Good News Club for a few months. Ms. Bateson enrolled me in a mail-in Bible School program which I faithfully completed. Afterward, I received a certificate and a "License to Preach." I had a great sense of accomplishment, to be only 13 years old with a "License to Preach." It wasn't an official ordination certificate or minister's license; it was a clever way to encourage the recipient to go out and fulfill the Great Commission. Back then I didn't think it could get any more official.

I look back and think of Ruth Bateson and how grateful I am for that little crippled missionary who had to leave her beloved mission field. She didn't use that as an excuse to retire from the Lord's call. She led her little Good News Club for many years and brought lots of kids (like me) to Jesus.

She also had a special phone setup on a gooseneck and had a *Dial-a-Prayer* line, through which she prayed for children and led many to Christ. Some of them later became pastors, evangelists, and missionaries. In several of my visits to her home, I sat and listened to her lovingly pray with callers. I can't even imagine the rewards that were stored up for her in heaven! What a powerful example for all of us to follow!

...that if you confess with your mouth the Lord Jesus and believe in your heart that God has raised Him from the dead, you will be saved.

Romans 10:9 NKJV

Chapter 9

A Spiritual Father

Ruth Bateson encouraged me to attend church at Calvary Assembly of God, which was only a couple of blocks from my house. It had a large youth ministry called The Rock House. Every week about 500 plus teenagers and young adults gathered to worship the Lord and hear teaching. Most of them were from the hippy culture, who had recently been saved and became part of the "Jesus Movement" which swept through Central Florida much as it did in Southern California.

It was also the height of the "Charismatic Movement," of which Calvary Assembly was a prominent part. In fact, Calvary Assembly was named the fastest growing church in America around that time and was holding five services on Sundays.

Ms. Bateson had some rental property behind her house, and one of her tenants was a draftsman named Burton Carey. She asked him if he would pick me up and take me to church. He graciously agreed and is still one of the humblest, loving, most gracious men I have ever met. He now serves as a missionary to the elderly.

I walked into an auditorium packed-out with metal folding chairs. People in jeans and t-shirts were singing and clapping. There was a full band on stage... drums, bass, acoustic and electric guitars, piano, organ and singers. I'd never seen anything like it. I imagine my eyes were bugged out the entire time. People were clapping and lifting their hands as they sang. It was so strange and so wonderful all at the same time.

After the singing, a man came out and began to teach the Bible in a way that even someone like me could understand. He did it with such joy and enthusiasm that I couldn't get enough. His name was Alex Clattenburg. At the time, I was told, he was a multi-millionaire real estate executive, who was responsible for selling the land that Walt Disney World sits on today. He had volunteered his time to serve as the youth pastor of The Rock House. He trained and discipled a group of men who served full-time as youth pastors for this large ministry. Pastor Alex would later baptize me, and he always made me feel loved and valued. He had the most loving, penetrating eyes, and when he spoke it was as if his eyes were looking right inside you. He is still pastoring at Church in the Son, in Orlando, Florida.

On the stage there was a tall, thin, young man with long straight hair parted down the middle, with wire-framed glasses, playing an acoustic guitar and leading the singing. I didn't know who he was at the time, but right then and there I determined that was what I wanted to do.

A few weeks later I met him. His name was Robert David Spradley. He was one of the youth pastors, responsible for the high school aged kids. We ended up in the church restroom at the same time. I looked at him and said, "I'm a minister too." He looked at me kind of amused, which I interpreted as impressed. He said, "Oh really? Why don't you come and see me this week on Tuesday, after school?" I can't even describe how excited I was that this cool guy, who played guitar and preached the gospel wanted to meet with me!

Tuesday arrived and I packed a briefcase with anything I thought might impress him, such as my "License to Preach" certificate and

50   I'm Taking You Another Way

some drawings I had done of the Lone Ranger and Batman. I rode my bike up to the church and he came out and welcomed me into his office. He asked me some questions and I told him some stories. I showed him the contents of my briefcase.

I don't remember any details of that first meeting. All I know is that despite my hokey drawings and my little certificate, he saw something in me that I couldn't see myself. That day we started a relationship that is still strong today. In many ways Robert became a father figure to me. He discipled me, not only in ministry, but in life. He taught me what it means to be a godly man, and a loving husband and father. Robert has a strong gift of leadership on his life. I would even say that it is apostolic.

That day was a real milestone in my life, and the start of many adventures. Robert welcomed me into his ministry and calling, also into his home and family. He included me in his personal life and created opportunities for me to develop my gifts. He was a constant source of encouragement, and still is even now. In fact, he was one of the first people to urge me to write this book. Be forewarned, Robert's name will come up several times in my story going forward! He was and is such an integral part of my life.

A person that is not mentioned as often but has also had a huge impact in my world is Robert's wife, Diana Spradley. Everything Robert has done, given, and included me in has been with the cooperation and consent of Diana. I could not even begin to count the number of delicious meals and desserts she prepared with me in mind. Diana readily accepted me into her life as much as Robert did. She doesn't get near the recognition and praise she deserves.

I have to tell a story that is chronologically out of sequence but fits in describing the type of person Diana is. Many years ago, while our daughter Grace was still a small baby, I was giving Robert and

Diana's son, Jesse, weekly guitar lessons in their home. They agreed to pay me $10 per lesson. At that time, Margie and I were really struggling financially, and that $10 made a big difference.

One week after giving Jesse his lesson, Robert came home and forgot to pay me. I was too ashamed to remind him, so I started to leave to head back home. At that point we were very low on baby formula and groceries, and I didn't know what I was going to do. We were really counting on that money. After driving a few miles, I decided that I could not go home and face Margie and my sweet little baby daughter empty handed. I swallowed my pride and turned around and headed back to the Spradley's house. I knocked on the door and they invited me in. They were all sitting at the table getting ready to eat supper. Robert asked, "What's going on, Jeff?"

Before I could answer, Diana looked at me and asked, "Jeff, do you have any food?" I looked down in shame trying not to cry and shook my head. She immediately jumped up from the table and grabbed a bunch of grocery bags and began to empty her refrigerator. Then she got some more bags and told me to follow her outside to the garage. She then began to empty her second refrigerator and freezer as well. She said, "Now you take this food, and you better let me know if you ever need food!"

Diana was usually quiet, but never a push-over. She looked at Robert and asked, "Did you remember to pay Jeff?" Robert pulled out his wallet, and she insisted that he give me double pay.

I will never forget what she did for me and my family that day. Even as I am writing this, my heart is flooded with emotion.

Even though Diana seldom comes up in this book, she was right there, and was always my advocate. I love her dearly and think of her as my spiritual mother.

For though you might have ten thousand instructors in Christ, yet you do not have many fathers; for in Christ Jesus I have begotten you through the gospel.

1 Corinthians 4:15 NKJV

Chapter 10

The Making of a Psalmist

After meeting Robert and being exposed to the playing of acoustic guitars in worship, I knew that was what I HAD to do. The only problems were, I didn't know how to play, and I didn't have a guitar to learn on. But I was undeterred!

Robert left his guitar out on the stage during the week. With his permission, I went to the church every afternoon after school to figure it out. I never considered taking lessons and they probably wouldn't have worked for me with my learning style. I sat there daily in the darkened auditorium and figured out how to play some chords. I also watched other players like a hawk to try to decipher what their fingers were doing. I did this for hours, even when my fingers started bleeding. It took a while, but eventually I was able to play a couple of songs. I sold my Honda dirt bike to buy my own guitar, which really helped speed up my learning process.

I've always said, "The number one ingredient you must have to become proficient on guitar is 'determined desire.'" This will carry you past the weeks and months of frustration trying to make your fingers do what feels unnatural and the discomfort of building callouses. I still have that determined desire!

Songwriting was also a big part of the worship at The Rock House. Members on the worship team wrote most of songs we sang every week. A lot of those songs were Scriptures set to modern music. Some of those worship team members had a huge impact on me. People like Robert, Gary Ramey, Rick Bussey, Rick Cox, and Jeannie Clattenburg regularly introduced new songs. They were my role models. We all went around singing those Scripture songs throughout the day (which is a great way to "hide the Word in your heart!").

With this flowing river of new songs, it became an expectation that if you played guitar or piano, you also wrote songs. I began as a young teenager to come up with my own. I've probably written over two hundred songs since those days (I've lost count). That may sound impressive but honestly, only about one third of them are any good (if that).

One of the greatest encouragers in my development as a music minister and songwriter was (surprise) Rob Spradley. He would often ask if I'd written anything new lately. Then he would sit and patiently listen as I played it for him. He never criticized but only encouraged me to keep writing more.

His expectations of me placed a demand on my gift. I would have never been sufficiently motivated to learn to play guitar and write songs if it was only going to be a hobby. If God had given me a gift, I was determined to put it to use for Him. Later in my life, my songwriting has had seasons of being prolific, as well as being reduced to barely a trickle. What usually made the difference was whether or not a demand was placed on the gift... whether I was in a situation where there was a need for something new and fresh.

I didn't start out leading worship up on stage. That came about in a less-direct way. Initially, Robert asked me to run the overhead projector during worship. To do so, I would stand next to one of those old-timey projectors and place a transparency sheet with lyrics written on it so that the congregation could see the words and sing along. Robert would normally pick four or five songs for a worship time out from one of those old accordion files and place them in order for me. But it was pretty much a foregone conclusion that he wasn't going to stick with the song list, and was going to stray into other songs not planned. The person responsible for running the projector had to be in tune with what was going on, and to be able to change or find the appropriate transparency sheets quickly.

By the grace of God, I developed the ability to anticipate when Robert was about to change gears, and even guess which song he was about to do. This seemingly unrelated area of service is something God used to prepare me for the ministry of a psalmist. It involved knowing which key the songs were in, as well as sensing when the Holy Spirit was moving in a different direction and moving with Him.

Another area of serving I'll mention...when Robert played a guitar, he played with gusto! He strummed with his whole arm, not his wrist. That resulted in frequent broken guitar strings. It became a common joke to say that we would gauge the "anointing" of a worship time based on how many strings he would break. I heard someone say, "Robert doesn't just play guitar, he assaults it!" Anyway, I learned to change strings and tune a guitar quickly, like a pit crew mechanic for a NASCAR race.

Looking back, it was those years of serving, running the overhead projector and changing another person's guitar strings, that God used to launch me into my own ministry.

Through the years, the Lord has opened many wonderful doors of music ministry for me. At age 17, for three days I had the privilege of leading worship for Benny Hinn at one of the Orlando Jesus Festivals. At this particular event, there was a main arena and three large circus tents that could seat between three to five thousand people each. There were various Bible teachers ministering each afternoon in all of the tents. I was assigned to the tent where Benny was one of the teachers. He was the son-in-law of my pastor, Dr. Roy Harthern, so he came to our church often. In the middle of my worship set, Benny came up, touched my shoulder and motioned for me to stop for a second. He said, "Everybody lift your hands and say, 'Jesus, come and touch me now!'" I then witnessed most, if not every person, inside our giant packed-out tent fall down under the power of the Holy Spirit. I even looked outside one of the tent flaps and saw a man carrying lawn chairs fall forward. As far as I could tell, there was not a single person standing, except Benny and me. I was holding on to my guitar protectively in case I was going down too. I looked at him and whispered, "What should I do?" He smiled and said very kindly, "Just keep playing, brother," which I did. After the three days of meetings, I went to shake his hand. He looked me over and said, "You're a pretty big fella. I'll see you again sometime, eh?"

In the years since, I've been honored to work with, open for, and lead worship for many well-known Christian artists and ministers. It has been the favor and kindness of God to allow me these opportunities. I give Him all the glory! I'm convinced that it's also related to faithfully serving another man's ministry, unnoticed by others, but seen by Him who holds the keys to our future and destiny!

And if you have not been faithful in what is another man's,
who will give you what is your own?

Luke 16:12 NKJV

Chapter 11

Man Makers

As long as I can remember, my favorite sport has been basketball. I loved meeting some of the church maintenance staff in the afternoons to shoot some hoops on the outside basketball court. One of the maintenance staff was a man named Rick Cox. He was a small man, but he was a very good basketball player and so fast and sneaky we called him "Tricky Ricky." He would often resort to distracting someone by pulling down their shorts on the court in order to steal the ball. I was his favorite victim and it happened often. The sad thing about it was, I never saw it coming. Despite him deriving great pleasure from my public humiliation, he and his wife Debi remain dear friends to this day. Rick was also a huge influence upon my guitar playing. I think of him as my older brother in Christ. I could never repay his and Debi's hospitality, kindness, and great patience with me.

The church started a high school city league basketball team, and Robert urged me to try out for the team. He thought it would help me get in shape and teach me some much-needed lessons about teamwork. By this time, I was in 11th grade and 6 feet 4 inches tall and about 240 pounds. Practices were on Monday nights, so I showed up for the tryout.

There were a number of high school boys there that night. Most of them had played organized sports before. Most all were much more athletic than me and some were even taller and could easily dunk a basketball. I was intimidated to say the least. The coach was Val Rodriguez, a big guy in his late 20's. Val was one of those guys you would call a "man's man." He was born to be a coach and he had the gift of motivation. He was most definitely someone you didn't want to get on the wrong side of. The other boys and I were all shooting around when Coach Val blew his whistle and told us to line up. We each started doing some layup drills, foul shots, and then dribbling down the court, weaving in and out. He was assessing each boy's ball handling skills. Then Coach Val told us to line up on the base line (the extreme end of the basketball court). He said that we were going to run some "man makers." I'd never heard of "man makers" before, but I remember thinking that this couldn't be good.

We were to start on the base line, run to the closest foul line, run back to the base line, run to the half court line, run back to the base line, run to the opposite foul line, then run back to the base line, run to the opposite end base line, then run all the way back to where we had started. I know now why they call them "man makers." They are terrible enough to make a grown man cry! I'm pretty sure they originated in the pit of hell, and if you go there, the devil will make you run them for eternity! Some may call them, "man makers," but I think they ought to be called "man killers!" I can't imagine they would even put Navy Seals through that kind of abuse!

We all lined up and Coach Val blew his whistle. We took off. About a quarter of the way through, I realized this was an ill-conceived and terrible idea. Right then and there I pretty much decided that I didn't even like basketball anymore. I was slower than everyone else and I felt deeply embarrassed along with feeling like my body was going to spontaneously combust right there on the court.

Everyone finished and I was still only about halfway through. I decided that after this practice was over, I was going to get on my bicycle and leave, never to come back. The only thing more painful than the burning in my stomach, lungs, and legs was the sense of shame. I didn't look, but I imagined everyone was laughing at me, and the coach was rolling his eyes. I was about two thirds of the way through when something unexpected happened. I felt a hand on my back. It was Coach Val. He said, "Come on, Jeff, I'll run it with you, you can do this!" Suddenly I felt a surge of strength and I was able to keep going. Then, following Coach's example, the other boys all ran onto the court and finished the last two rounds with me. I will never forget what Coach Val and the other boys did that evening. Val cared more about me than anything that I could do for him. His team followed his example.

That season, our team, The Rock House Sons, won the city league championship and a post season tournament. I was a third-string center. Coach Val would normally put me in to take up room in the lane, so that the other players could drive around me and score. On occasion, Coach Val would yell out, "ABT!" which stood for "atomic butt thrust" (my signature move). This would be when one of our guys was driving to the basket, I would step in between our guy and whoever was guarding him. I would then sweep my enormous backside toward the opponent, moving them out of the way. I got a lot of fouls called on me, but it helped a few of our guys to score.

By the way, during that regular season I didn't score a single point. But in our final tournament game, Coach Val put me in the last two minutes of the game. He told the team to get me the ball. I went in like a bull in a china shop. I played with so much intensity I got four fouls called on me in less than two minutes!

While the other team was shooting their foul shots, Coach Val sent me toward the opposite end of the court. The foul shot was rebounded by one of our guys, and they threw a long pass to me as I was all alone at the other end of the court. I caught the pass and only had a few steps to go to make a layup before the buzzer sounded. One guy got down the court to defend the basket. I somehow faked him out to go another direction, then I did a reverse layup on the left side of the rim, and it went in!!!! Dr. J (Julius Irving) would have been impressed (I think). The buzzer sounded and my team rushed on the court as if I'd scored the winning basket in the NCAA National Championship (we were up by 22 points already). They all picked me up on their shoulders (no easy feat) and carried me to the sidelines. Then they started dancing and making up some funny song about me. Oh, the glory and triumph of that moment!

Back to the man makers... Val Rodriguez taught me so much about character and integrity and has been a tremendous gift to my life. That first evening, when all I wanted to do was quit and go somewhere private and cry, he demonstrated what Jesus does for each of us. Jesus doesn't always take us out of our troubles, and He doesn't stand on the sidelines shaking His head in disgust at our pathetic performance. No, He comes alongside of us and puts His hand on our back and says, *"I'll run this with you. You can do this!"*

I have strength for all things in Christ Who empowers me [I am ready for anything and equal to anything through Him Who infuses inner strength into me; I am self-sufficient in Christ's sufficiency].

Philippians 4:13 AMP

Chapter 12

Flew the Coop

Back on the home front... the environment at my home was still pretty negative. But now that I was older and spent more time away, it wasn't so bad. I got a job working at a local music store after school. I worked in the warehouse pulling orders for customers, doing inventory and shipping and receiving. It was the premiere music store in Central Florida at that time. They provided all the rental sound and lighting for Walt Disney World also. It was a busy but enjoyable place to work. Also, it felt good to earn some money and to be around music gear at the same time.

During my time at Edgewater High School, I didn't take my studies very seriously. I made grades that were good enough to pass. It wasn't even on my radar to attend college after graduation. I was there to get through it and to tell others about Jesus.

I took a failing grade in speech class because the teacher wouldn't allow me to give my final grade "persuasive speech." I had intended to prove, in my final speech, that Jesus is who He says He is. I used some of the wonderful material from Josh McDowell's great book *Evidence that Demands a Verdict*. My prepared written speech created such a fuss that it ended up being taken to the school board. Though I wasn't allowed to give it, there were people that read it. Perhaps the Lord planted some seeds in their hearts.

During junior high and high school, I spent my lunch breaks outside, preaching to the other kids about Jesus. A few of the students who came out to laugh and make fun of me ended up giving their hearts to Jesus and became dedicated followers of Christ.

Upon graduation, my parents bought me my own car, a '62 Chevrolet Impala. It was light blue with lots of rust. It had electric windows that didn't work and neither did the air conditioner... not a good combination in hot, sunny Florida. But it got me off of a bicycle and I loved it! If the car went over 35 mph, it would start shaking, so I mainly stuck to side roads rather than using I-4 (the main highway through Orlando).

With my new wheels, I was able to get another job a little further away. I ended up working at a resort apartment complex called Spanish Trace, in nearby Altamonte Springs. I was a porter, which means I kept the parking lot and hallways clean. It was an enjoyable job, plus I got to work with some fun characters and ride around on golf carts.

One Sunday, Robert and Diana Spradley invited me out to lunch after the church service. We (along with their two children) went to Pondarosa Steakhouse. During the meal, Robert said that they were moving. He had accepted a position as a youth pastor at a church in Charleston, South Carolina. At that time, the church was known as Northwood Assembly of God. Robert explained a little about the process that brought him and Diana to conclude that this was what God wanted for their family. I quietly listened to every word and when Rob finished, he asked, "What do you think Jeff?"

I looked Robert in the eye and without hesitation said, "I'm going with you." It wasn't even something I had to think about. It wasn't anything I could see coming either. All I knew was that wherever he was going, I was going too!

He said, "Okay then." On the way to drop me off at my home, he talked about going up ahead of me and finding me a job and a place to live. Sure enough, three months later he found me a job with a man in the church, and it came with an apartment to live in. I packed my few belongings in my car and headed out! My mother had said to me a few times over the years, "I can't wait until you turn 18 and get out of this house. I'm tired of having to feed you and put up with you!" I never responded back to her, but ended up leaving home at 17, ahead of schedule. She seemed to regret saying those words.

The title of this chapter is "Flew the Coop," which is an idiom that uses a chicken metaphor, meaning someone has left a place or situation of confinement that limits their freedom. That's what I did at 4:00 one morning, after first having a quick breakfast with my friend David. David was a young man, one year older than me, who was my guitar playing buddy. In fact, he had received an inheritance at the age of 18 and used some of it to buy the both of us guitars. He even let me pick mine out... now that's a friend!

My parents loaned me a newer, more reliable car to take up to South Carolina. I'd never driven that far in my life! Charleston was about six and a half hours from Orlando, and somewhere on the early morning drive, in Georgia, I fell asleep at the wheel. I woke up with my car about to swerve into the median on I-95. I awoke in a panic and was able to gain control of the vehicle and steer it back into the lane. The road was pretty sparse at that time of morning, thank God! I came to a rest area, went in, splashed water on my face and did a couple of push-ups to make sure I was alert for the rest of the trip.

If falling asleep at the wheel has ever happened to you, you know the heart-pounding sense of terror I'm writing about. I believe the devil wanted to thwart what God had planned for me in this new place. I also believe God's angels were assigned to get me there. This was not the first time angels have come to my rescue...

JEFFERY L. STOCKFORD

A few years before this, when I was about 13, I left the Bible bookstore near my house and was crossing a busy street on my 10-speed bicycle. The light changed while I was in the middle of the intersection. Suddenly, my bicycle chain popped off and I fell down into the street on my left side, straddling my bike. I looked up to see a car barreling toward me. I didn't have time to move. I squeezed my eyes shut and raised my arm to brace for impact. Amazingly, it seemed nothing happened. When I opened my eyes, I found myself lying in the grass on the opposite side of the six-lane road (Edgewater Drive), still straddling my bicycle! There is absolutely no way, naturally speaking, I could have gotten there on my own. I believe it had to have been angels swooping in to move me out of harm's way. I am very thankful for His angels' work in my life!

Are not all the angels ministering spirits sent out [by God] to serve (accompany, protect) those who will inherit salvation? [Of course they are!]

Hebrews 1:14 AMP

Chapter 13

My World Just Got Bigger

I arrived in Charleston, unpacked my car, and began a new season of life, out on my own for the first time. Robert helped me in getting set up with phone service and electricity in my name. I have to say that I was unprepared for such a big step. I'd never learned about balancing a checkbook and being disciplined with money. There were a lot of financial lessons I learned the hard way. But God has always been faithful to provide for all my needs, despite my short sightedness and foolishness.

I met a very remarkable man when I arrived, who would become one of the biggest difference makers in my life. His name was Fred Richard, and he was the senior pastor of Northwood Assembly. Everyone called him Pastor Fred (I still do). He is one of the most unique and godly men I've ever been exposed to.

Fred was from Texas, and like Coach Val, was a "man's man." Pastor Fred was a former All-American football player. He was a bit intimidating, kind of gruff, and spoke what he was thinking without the slightest hint of sugar-coating. Underneath that tough exterior, he had a tender heart of gold. I later came to really love and appreciate him, and I believe that despite many episodes of goofiness and stupid moves on my part, he was committed to loving me. I hold him in my heart with the highest respect.

Pastor Fred and his wife Soni had three children: two boys and one little girl. Her name was Carmen. Before we arrived in Charleston, Carmen had developed brain cancer, when she was seven or eight years old. They took her to doctors who offered no real hope. They took her to some of the prominent healing evangelists, but they wouldn't even pray for her. In fact, one of them smugly said Carmen was sick because of her parents' lack of faith.

Through all this heartbreak, Pastor Fred faithfully served his church, teaching, counseling, and praying for the sick, etc. One day he received the call that Carmen had passed on to heaven. He rushed home and arrived before the EMS got there. He walked in and saw his precious daughter's lifeless body. He picked her up and carried her out into the backyard. He lifted her to God and said, "This doesn't change anything God. I'm still going to love You and serve You, the best I can."

That day something changed in the atmosphere between heaven and earth. Northwood Assembly began to grow exponentially, and a sovereign move of God began to take place there. With the influx of new people coming in, Pastor Fred knew that he needed help in the area of youth. God had given him the name "Robert Spradley" in his spirit during prayer, so he researched until he found him. He then invited Robert and Diana to Charleston to partner with him and the other ministers there.

Robert established a ministry to middle-schoolers through young adults and called it YouthQuake. Nothing like that had ever happened in that area, and in a short time, there were about three hundred young people worshipping and being discipled. YouthQuake made a huge impact on that region, along with Northwood Assembly.

I moved there as the "tide was beginning to rise." I was invited to oversee the praise and worship and put together a band. We called it the Youthquake Band. We led worship every week and even performed in churches around North and South Carolina from time to time.

There was a particular event during this time that helped shape my solo music ministry. Northwood Assembly also had a Christian school. Every Friday, Robert would lead a chapel service for the junior high and high school students. I assisted by leading worship. I worked for the school in the mornings as a physical education teacher (which is kind of a joke because I spent most of my school years trying to get out of P.E.). I then worked for the youth ministry in the afternoons.

One week I was asked to do a concert for the school's chapel service. The night before, I went up to the church to set up my music equipment and to practice. I began to play and worship there in the darkened sanctuary. I asked the Lord if there was anything He wanted me to say. I believe He said (in my spirit) to tell them, *"Some of you who claim to be Christians are really white-washed tombs full of dead men's bones."* That seemed like a strange thing to say to a group of middle and high school students. I thought it was a little over their heads, but I obeyed the Lord. The next morning in the chapel service, after doing some of my funny material and telling a few stories, I gave them the message. As soon as I did, something unexpected and phenomenal happened!

The strong awareness of the presence of God fell upon that room. Kids started crying and lifting their hands. Some came up to the altar in repentance and knelt in God's presence. Several were born-again that morning. The only way I can describe it was that it was a sovereign move of the Holy Spirit.

The chapel service went much longer than the allotted hour, but they didn't shut it down. Teachers were praying with students, and it seemed nobody wanted to leave. The school schedule was altered for the rest of the day.

The outpouring of the Holy Spirit in that chapel service spilled over into the youth ministry during the following weeks. We saw many apathetic, hard-hearted young people fall in love with Jesus and commit their lives to Him!

Doors began to open for me to go out and sing and share with other churches, youth groups, and camps around the region. I got to see a similar kind of outpouring of the Holy Spirit in many of those meetings. It was a wonderful season in my life, and to this day, I still enjoy getting an opportunity to travel to churches to sing and "brag on Jesus." It is my favorite thing to do!

Those years at Northwood Assembly were very formative, where my leadership, musicianship, and calling were developed. But more important than any of those things was some much-needed character development.

And Jabez called on the God of Israel saying,
"Oh, that You would bless me indeed,
and enlarge my territory,
that Your hand would be with me, and that You
would keep me from evil, that I may not cause pain!"
So God granted him what he requested.

1 Chronicles 4:10 NKJV

Chapter 14

A Painful Lesson

One of the things I've learned is that singing and playing on a worship team/band is a position of leadership. Leaders are to be held to a higher standard. By virtue of being up front on the stage, they are examples, either for good or bad. So, part of my leadership responsibility in YouthQuake, in addition to the music and worship aspects, was to pastor the band members. That wasn't a hard job, because most of them were already devoted to Jesus and following Him with all their hearts.

From time to time one of the band members would get involved in situations which would require some biblical correction, and on a few occasions, I had to ask them to sit out for a while, until they were able to work through their issues. That was the most difficult part of my job. I'm not a confrontational person by nature.

Robert, on the other hand, had no problem with that aspect. More times than I can remember, he sat me down to confront issues or bad attitudes in me. Somewhere in the session he would usually point his (long, bony) finger at me and say something like, "Jeff, don't you ever do that again!" He believed God's hand was on my life and didn't want me to disqualify myself by harboring a bad attitude or some other character flaw.

In fact, one time I got frustrated with him doing that so often. I didn't see him doing that to the other men who served on the leadership team. His answer disarmed me and melted my resistance. He said, "Jeff, you wanna know why I correct you so often? That's because I expect more from my son than I do from the kid down the street."

One of those times I had asked our drummer to take a break for a few weeks. Doing so, I had to find a replacement. You can't have a rock-n-roll band without a drummer! Another drummer had started attending YouthQuake around that same time. He seemed like a good guy to fill in. He even had "Jesus is Lord" printed on his bass drum. He joined us and did a great job and we even considered making him a permanent part of the band.

One day Robert and I were driving downtown, and he informed me that some of the kids in the youth group had witnessed this new drummer drinking alcohol the previous weekend. He said, "You know what you need to do. We can't have someone on our worship team setting that kind of example." I swallowed hard and agreed that I would talk to him about it. This guy was older than me and I really didn't want to confront someone I felt a little inferior to. So, I never followed up and talked to him. I had intended to, but it never seemed like a good time.

Several weeks later, the shocking news came that this young man had committed suicide in his mother's garage. We didn't know it at the time, but he had metal plates surgically placed in his head from a childhood condition, and in his later years this caused him terrible pain. One night the pain became so great that he must have snapped and took his life with a shotgun.

It sent shock waves through our tight-knit youth group. A few days after the funeral, Robert asked me to go to lunch with him. We met at one of my favorite spots, Western Sizzlin' Steakhouse.

I loaded up my plate with all my favorites and we sat down together in the back of the restaurant. Robert asked me if I had ever followed through in meeting with this brother. I had to say that I had not. He then, with an all-too-familiar serious face, said, "Jeff, you should have pushed through your self-consciousness and been involved in his life." Then came the words that broke my heart, "Who knows, but maybe you could have made a difference and he might even be alive today." That was like a punch to the gut, and instantly tears with uncontrollable sobs with snot came out all over my shirt and plate. That is one of the few times in my life I wasn't able to eat. I don't think I heard anything Robert said after that. I left the restaurant still sobbing and drove to the cemetery.

I sat there on the ground in front of his grave. I wept and wept some more. I prayed and told God I was sorry for shirking my responsibility to care enough for this young man to get involved in his life beyond playing in the band. I also apologized to this brother. I don't know if people in heaven can hear us here on earth, but I spoke to him as if he could.

I went home and decided that I was going to leave and head back to Orlando. Overwhelmed with a sense of failure, shame, and uselessness, I believed things would never be the same between Robert and me. I started packing my belongings and was planning to leave without telling anybody. Then my phone rang.

The person on the other end was my great friend, Jim Kelly. We became friends as teenagers in Orlando. We played guitar together for hours at a time, and a little basketball too. He had moved to Charleston to work with Robert and me. He led the middle-school ministry of YouthQuake. He called out of the blue to check on me. I told him what happened and that I was going to leave that night. He expressed his love and asked me to reconsider.

He must have snitched on me (for a good reason) because a few minutes later, Robert called to reaffirm his love for me and to let me know that I was very valuable to him, and he wanted me to stay. I decided to remain there, and this was never mentioned again, although I've had to be corrected for many other things since then.

Some might think that what Robert said to me that day was unfair. After all, how could anyone know what this poor tormented young man was driven to do that terrible night?

Looking back, I don't think what Robert said was unfair or unwarranted. He was using that as an opportunity to stress the importance of being more than a band leader and a buddy to the other musicians. I needed a "shepherd's heart" for them as well. Pastoral leadership in the body of Christ is going to sometimes include <u>loving</u> confrontation and administering correction. It is never comfortable, but it is a necessary part of the job I signed up for. With God's help, I've learned how to do that when I had to. Not perfectly, but understanding the stakes are too high to allow destructive behavior to continue without addressing it in love.

Ultimately, I am deeply thankful to Robert for loving me enough to confront me when I veered off the right path. He cared enough to step in and pull me back from the brink.

I am also thankful for my life-long friend, Jim Kelly, who has more than once stepped in when I was hurting and confused. He has always listened without judging and has been someone God has used as a healing balm in my life.

Whoever loves instruction loves knowledge,
but he who hates correction is stupid.

Proverbs 12:1 NKJV

Chapter 15

My Little Buddy

A special friend entered my life in the final year or so that I lived in Charleston. His name was Mark Shiver. I first noticed him in our YouthQuake meetings sitting near the front row. When I went up on stage at the end of a message to play guitar softly, as Robert was giving some kind of challenge or altar call, I would glance over to my left and see this short, portly dude with a mustache and puffy hair, sitting with his hands folded on his stomach, with his eyes closed. I was convinced that he was sleeping although he insisted that he was deep in prayer.

I needed a new roommate situation, so I put the word out. Mark came up to me after the service one Sunday night and said that he was looking for a roommate as well. He rented a two-bedroom duplex and we moved in together. We were cut from the same cloth as far as humor goes... both over-the-top silly and pranksters.

One time we decided that there were some single young adult ladies that were not as respectful to us as we thought they should be. They needed some discipline! We formed a duo called "Women Disciplers, International." Mark and I would go around to various homes of these "uppity" girls and put petroleum jelly on their car door handles late at night, which they would discover the next morning on their way to work or class. It was the kind of thing that might get someone arrested or shot these days.

One day we recorded about ten minutes of the two of us laughing hysterically on a cassette tape. We put about a five-minute leader on the front end of the recording. Late one night we went to the mobile home of two of the YouthQuake ladies, and duct-taped a cheap cassette player with the laughing tape in it, to one of their bedroom windows. We hit "play" and ran and hid. With great delight, in the distance, we could hear the irritating laughter start, the lights came on, and shadows began frantically running back and forth in front of the windows until they discovered the source. Looking back, it was a pretty stupid thing to do, but stupid things were our specialty!

All these young ladies we "Vaselined" got their revenge. On my last Sunday in Charleston, they filled my car up with shrimp. They even stuffed shrimp in my car's air vents. They also hid some under the sun visor, which fell out onto my lap when I lowered it a few days later. Did I mention I can't stand shrimp or any kind of seafood? So, I was the one who got "discipled." The smell never left my '76 Grand Prix. Eventually I wrecked it and it ended up at the salvage yard. The moral of that story is, "People, lock your cars!"

I could write a whole book about the misadventures of Mark and me. But he was much more than a funny prankster partner in crime. He has been a true friend to me. I consider him the brother I never really got to have.

Later on, I moved to Raleigh, North Carolina, along with Robert Spradley, Jim Kelly, Noel Cookman, Russ Parker and Ron Body to help plant a new church. Mark Shiver joined us a few months later and we picked up where we left off as roommates, with slightly fewer shenanigans.

A few years down the road, Mark was still in Raleigh, and I had moved back to Charleston for reasons that I'll expand on later. But

I thought I'd mention a special event here. I felt the Lord had laid it upon my heart to meet with Mark to commemorate our friendship. We decided to meet in Myrtle Beach one afternoon. I drove up from Charleston and he drove down from Raleigh. We met at a place called "The Filling Station," which was an all-you-can-eat buffet with a pizza bar, a make your own sub bar, salad bar, dessert bar, etc. Our kind of place! We ate a hearty meal and put a hurtin' on 'em, and then drove to the beach and walked out on the beach. It wasn't crowded at that time of year.

I told Mark that I wanted to make a "covenant" with him. Basically, that I would commit to a life-long friendship with him, and I'd never let him fall away from Christ without stepping in to prevent that from happening. My exact biblical terminology was flawed, but I meant it from the heart. If I had known that an actual biblical covenant involved some bloodshed, I might have chosen a different term. We both committed to each other, and we've been there for each other through the years, ups and downs, failures and triumphs. Our commitment continues to this day, and I am so thankful for my "covenant" brother in Christ!

In today's church, some call this kind of commitment "accountability." But I've never cared much for that term. It sounds like a legal term for which someone stands over you to keep you in check. But the Bible does not teach that we are to hold one another "accountable." However, it does teach us to bear one another's burdens.

Bear one another's burdens, and so fulfill the law of Christ.

Galatians 6:2 NKJV

Bearing one another's burdens communicates that we are brothers, helping one another to the end. It reminds me of many of the races and marathons I've seen, where someone has collapsed or is about to collapse from exhaustion. Another runner comes alongside of them, helps them to their feet, puts the weary runner's arm over their own shoulder, and helps them to cross the finish line.

Then Jonathan and David made a covenant,
because he loved him as his own soul.

1 Samuel 18:3 NKJV

Chapter 16

I Didn't See That Coming

The entire team that was headed to Raleigh to plant a new church for God's glory was very excited. There was a strong sense of purpose and destiny amongst us. We all believed God was going to do incredible things for us and through us! All the planning for that first introductory service came together better than we had imagined.

We rented the ballroom of the Raleigh Hilton (downtown). Phil Driscoll, the great trumpet player and singer, agreed to come do a concert and plug the new church, on Sunday, June 24, 1984. The ballroom was packed with over 800 people. I led a few worship songs at the beginning, then Phil Driscoll came up and blew the audience away! He encouraged the people who were looking for a new church to come and check out Raleigh Christian Community.

The next Sunday evening, the meeting was moved to the downstairs banquet room next to the bar. Out of the 800 plus attenders the week before, about 40 people returned. We had a core with which to start a church. Over the next 20 years the church grew to be about 1200.

Those early days of RCC were both exciting and difficult. Planting a church requires a constant all-hands-on-deck mentality. It means wearing many different hats and doing whatever is necessary. I will add that another indispensable quality is "thick skin."

My role on the team was to lead worship, set up the sound equipment, tear it down afterward, and transport the PA equipment in a trailer. The equipment was quite heavy, and I had a cart to roll it into the hotel, and then onto the kitchen elevator. As the fledging church was getting off the ground, meeting and connecting with the visitors was crucial. Robert and the other team members were doing that before and after the service, while I dealt with setting up and breaking down the equipment. I should have been connecting with people as well, then maybe I could have recruited some helpers. However, I've always been task oriented, which can eventually lead to frustration and burn-out.

One week something was different. The kitchen staff had something going on upstairs in the ballroom and said we couldn't use the kitchen elevator. That meant that the heavy equipment had to be physically carried up and down the stairs. The hotel didn't want us to use the guest elevator, either. I managed to get all of the equipment downstairs and set up. But after the meeting, everyone sat around and chatted with the new attenders and amongst themselves. No one seemed to notice or care that I alone had the undesirable task of carrying all that heavy equipment up two flights of stairs. This made me angry, and a seed of offense began to grow in my heart.

At that time, I was living in the small basement apartment in Robert and Diana's house. Many of the church planting team had raised their own support, but I hadn't. The last year or so I had supported myself through my concert ministry. By that, I mean I was invited to other churches/youth groups/retreats/conferences, etc. to sing and share my testimony. Afterward I would normally receive an honorarium and sometimes travel expense reimbursements. I had put all that aside in order to be available to help with this new church, without thinking through how I would make a living. I soon started feeling the financial pressure, plus I knew I couldn't stay indefinitely in Robert's basement.

It was around this time I received an invitation to go out to Fort Worth, Texas to minister in music for a large church. I'd been there before and amazingly they wanted me back! In the past I'd always been encouraged to take advantage of these opportunities and I didn't see why this would be any different. I agreed to come, and the plane tickets were sent to me in the mail. I let Robert know when I would be back, and he agreed to give me a ride to RDU Airport.

I arrived in Texas and had a great time! The pastor that booked me also arranged for me to minister in some other places. One night I ministered at televangelist Robert Tilton's church in Dallas, and another evening I did a full concert at "Christ For the Nations." My amazing Texas drummer friend Mark Zaragoza joined me. Mark used to play for the groups "Rat" and "Survivor" in their early years back in Chicago. It was a super fun mini tour, and we had a glorious time! One of the few times in my life that I received a standing ovation happened that night at "Christ For the Nations." I was so pumped that I could have flown back to Raleigh without a plane. However, my arrival wasn't what I was expecting.

I'd given Robert my itinerary but when my flight arrived back in Raleigh, he wasn't there to pick me up. I waited and then ended up getting a cab back to the house. I assumed that if he dropped me off, he would pick me up. I was kind of irritated. But I don't remember specifically asking him to come and get me.

When I entered the basement, which had a separate entrance, Robert was there waiting for me. He didn't seem very excited about how well my trip went. Apparently, on the Sunday that I was gone, my responsibilities weren't covered there at church, which I honestly didn't even think of. He said that I needed to make up my mind whether I was going to pursue traveling around or commit to helping get the new church up and running. It turned into a heated argument and an ultimatum was given to me. The discussion ended with me deciding "I'm out!"

Now, years later, having been a lead pastor, I understand the importance of knowing who on your team is committed and who isn't. At that time, I wasn't able to place myself in Robert's shoes. If I could go back in time, I would have chosen differently.

I moved in with my buddy Mark Shiver who was now living in Raleigh and had an apartment in an unsavory area of town. He was patient while I looked for a job and kept me fed. Mark had moved to Raleigh to be part of the new church, but after that discussion with Robert in the basement, I'd decided that I wasn't going back. A root of bitterness began to grow in my heart from perceived offenses. Allowing these bitter roots to grow has cost me dearly throughout my life and sadly, this was certainly not the last time. Please understand, allowing bitterness in your heart will cost you dearly as well!

Over the next six months, my life went into a downhill spiral. I wrecked my car and ended up buying another one which I couldn't afford, only to have it repossessed. I turned it in to the bank when I couldn't make the payments, but it still went on my record as a repossession. Without transportation I couldn't get to my job at ITT Telcom, so I had to quit. Having no money, I hocked my beloved Martin guitar and the pawn shop only gave me $300. I was never able to get it back. My other guitar was an Ovation Classical that once belonged to Christian musical artist Scott Wesley Brown, who befriended me and was a huge inspiration and encouragement. Unfortunately, I hocked and lost that one too.

Back at my apartment, with no car, no job, and no guitar, I began sinking into a deep depression. I went in the backyard and burned all my promotional materials, promo photos, letterhead, etc. I couldn't see a way forward after all that had happened.

One evening I felt the urge to pray, but I was so discouraged I couldn't even mouth the words. I walked into the woods beside our apartment and wrote out my prayer on a piece of paper. I don't remember what my note to God said, but I'm pretty sure it wasn't filled with positive faith confessions. It was most likely extremely pitiful, but somehow, I felt like God heard me.

Five minutes after walking back into the apartment from the woods, the phone rang. On the other end was Pastor Fred Richard. He said that he was thinking about me. Before I could reply, he said, "Here's what's going to happen... I'm sending a young man with a pickup truck. He is going to get you and your stuff and bring you back here to Charleston. You are going to be our children's minister and you are going to help lead worship again for the YouthQuake service. We've bought you a used car and you can pay us back over time from your paycheck. We've got you a roommate and an apartment and we will pay you a salary. Any questions?"

I returned to Charleston and Northwood Assembly. After arriving, another thing was added to my job description. I, along with the current youth pastor, Barry Shropshier, who had taken Robert's place, were commissioned to do the "Bowl Patrol." That meant we cleaned the bathrooms for the church and for the Christian School. We called ourselves "Captain Commode and the Urinal Colonel." During the many years of serving in various positions, the "Bowl Patrol" has never been far removed from my ministry, even as a lead pastor.

Pastor Fred's act of extreme generosity and compassion, and the timing, could have only been inspired and orchestrated by God. I was one small step from living on the street and God intervened on my behalf. I spent the next eleven months in Charleston serving and receiving grace. But God's plan for my life redirected me back to Raleigh.

JEFFERY L. STOCKFORD 83

I waited patiently for the Lord to help me
and He turned to me and heard my cry.
He lifted me out of the pit of despair,
out of the mud and the mire.
He set my feet on solid ground and
steadied me as I walked along.

He has given me a new song to sing,
a hymn of praise to our God.
Many will see what He has done and be amazed.
They will put their trust in the Lord.

Psalm 40:1-3 NKJV

Chapter 17

The Love of My Life

While in Charleston the second time, Barry and I took the kids from YouthQuake to a huge youth event in Gatlinburg, Tennessee, called Snow Safari. It was a three-day conference with several other youth ministries combined. There were some big-name Christian bands and excellent speakers. Robert Spradley was the keynote speaker the first night. We had been somewhat estranged since that night in his basement where we parted ways. I was sitting way back in the convention center listening as he ministered powerfully. Then somewhere in his message, he referenced the lyrics to one of my songs and stated, "written by my dear friend, Jeff Stockford."

It was like he was extending a loving "olive branch" to me. After that night, I knew that my place was to be with him back in Raleigh. We were soon reconciled, and arrangements were made for me to return.

Another significant event took place during that conference in Gatlinburg. I'd not been very successful in any of my relationships with women. I'd been engaged twice, and both engagements fell apart. Any dating I did usually ended up with me feeling hurt and rejected. I thought perhaps that it wasn't in God's will for me to be married. One afternoon between sessions, I went into the darkened convention center and knelt down in prayer. I said, "Lord, I acknowledge Your right to keep me all to Yourself. If You don't want me to be married, that's okay. I'm Yours and not my own."

I stood up feeling as if I'd done something important. Later I learned that at that same retreat was a beautiful, strawberry-blonde haired young lady, who had prayed a similar prayer, dedicating herself to live single for the Lord, if that was what He wanted. That beautiful young lady was Margie Paschall LeGwin. Now she goes by the name Margie Stockford. She changed her name and marital status about a year or so later.

Shortly after the retreat I moved back to Raleigh and once again was a roommate with my little buddy Mark Shiver. The singles ministry at the church was having a retreat at Myrtle Beach, South Carolina, and I was invited to do a concert and lead worship at it. Another man whom I greatly admired was the speaker for the retreat, Greg Wigfield.

I pulled into the hotel where the retreat was being held and began to unload my luggage and guitar. All of a sudden, I looked up to see the aforementioned beautiful, strawberry-blonde young lady walking toward me. She came up to me and said, "Hi, my name is Margie." I couldn't fathom how someone so gorgeous would intentionally walk up to someone like me (not the most attractive man out there). She was (and still is) waaaaaaaay out of my league. All throughout that retreat I couldn't stop watching her. She worked at the book table at the back of the meeting room, and I had trouble concentrating on my ministry responsibilities with her standing back there. I was completely smitten!

Back in Raleigh I was hired to work at the church as the children's pastor and custodian, plus leading worship occasionally on Wednesday nights. I made a whopping salary of $150 per week before taxes. I wanted to ask Margie out on a date, but I couldn't afford it. I borrowed $10 from Robert, which I thought would be enough. I planned to ask her out to the Sunday brunch buffet at the Holiday Inn, which was advertised as being $5 per person.

I asked, and she said, "Yes." We chose to go the following Sunday after church. That brunch was the beginning of a somewhat rocky, five-month courtship. I was so taken with her that unfortunately I lost what little "cool" I had and kinda smothered her. Though she believed the Lord had said to her that I was her future husband, she could never bring herself to say, "I love you." I was completely in love with her from the start. I told her so every time I was with her. I even wrote about my love for her in a song. I would tell her I loved her, then I'd try to move on to another subject so that she wouldn't feel pressured to say it back. I somehow didn't get the memo of the whole "play it cool" part of dating. I'd previously heard one Bible teacher say, "Don't ever tell a girl you love her unless you're ready to say in the next breath, 'Will you marry me?'" Honestly, I was ready from day one!

After a few breakups, then reuniting, I eventually decided to back off and enjoy the relationship for what it was at that point in time. Not long after that, we were attending a church banquet together held at a nice hotel in town, when Margie said she wanted to talk with me about something. We drove to the church, which now had its own property of 52 acres. On the property there was a private pond with a small pier and a bench. We sat, and after a few minutes of silence, she took my hand and said, "I love you." I'd already determined that if she ever uttered those words, I'd propose to her on the spot. However, I wasn't expecting her to say it then. In fact, I thought maybe she wanted to break up with me.

But there it was, she said it! I was a little shocked and asked her to excuse me for a second. I got up and walked to the end of the pier. I prayed, "Lord, You heard her. You know what I'm going to do. You had better stop me because I can't stop myself!" I paused and then heard my Heavenly Father's voice in my spirit as clear as ever. He said, *"What are you waiting for?"*

I walked back to Margie still on the bench and "assumed the position." I got down on one knee and asked her to marry me. She said, "Yes."

The following week, Margie was going to visit her family in Wilmington, North Carolina for Easter. I knew I had to somehow get her an engagement ring before she left. I lived at that time, in Wendell, a little town outside of Raleigh. There was an old jewelry store there, called "Strict's Jewelers and Watch Repair." I didn't know how much diamond rings cost, but I was willing to use my entire paycheck of $150 to get one. I had a rude awakening! I told the elderly man (Mr. Strict) what I had. And he showed me some tiny little diamond rings. One stood out to me, a 1/10 of a carat diamond solitaire. He wanted $175 for it but I talked him down to my price. Incidentally I had zero credit due to that repossession a few years before. He agreed, and I walked out of that store with what I thought was a giant glistening rock in my pocket.

I made Margie a little Easter basket and put the ring inside a plastic egg. She found it and acted so surprised. I now think her surprise was that the ring was so small. But she was so gracious and sweet. She put it on her finger and wore it home. Looking back, I believe she wore it not because she was proud of it. She wore it because she loved me, and she knew that was the best I could do. In my defense, I really thought I'd done something great! After all, it took my entire paycheck, plus the ring seemed a lot bigger in the store.

We were engaged for five months and encountered a number of challenges with family members on her side, but we persevered through, and God worked everything out. On July 18, 1987, we stood side-by-side and were united in marriage, in a barn that the church had converted into the church sanctuary. The guests consisted of Margie's parents, her sister, Louisa, and a few other relatives. No one in my family came, so some of the church staff and members stood in as my family. My former bandmate, Brett Singleton came up from Charleston to be my best man. It was a simple and unrehearsed ceremony (which I don't recommend). Robert Spradley officiated and Jim Kelly prayed over us.

We had a simple reception and then we were off to honeymoon in the North Carolina mountains. It was the absolute best week of my entire life! As of the writing of this book, Margie and I have been married for 36 years. The Scripture at the end of this chapter has certainly proven to be true!

One of the bonuses of marrying Margie has been getting to be part of her family. They have been more of a family to me than the one I was born into. Although the question, "Where did you find him?" has come up numerous times through the years, they have pretty much accepted me, quirks and all. Louisa, my sweet, hilarious, delightful sister-in-law, is such a bright light in my life. There's always lots of laughs when she comes to visit Margie and me.

The man who finds a wife finds a treasure,
and he receives favor from the LORD.

Proverbs 18:22 NLT

Chapter 18

Drinking Poison

Now married, Margie and I began our new life together. Margie worked for the North Carolina State Treasurer's Office as an auditor. I continued to work at Raleigh Christian Community as the children's pastor and custodian. Life was going smoothly, and I was pretty much as happy as I'd ever been.

The relationship with Robert had become a little more complex. I look back now and think that was the normal strain between a (spiritual) father and son, as the son wants to find his own way and achieve some level of respect as his own man. We'd had some disagreements and a degree of tension from time to time, but nothing too serious. Robert is a Type-A personality whereas I'm somewhat the opposite, which on occasion caused us to rub each other the wrong way, resulting in a flare-up.

One day I went into the church office to get a check signed to purchase something needed for the children's ministry, called Boredom Blasters. The church administrator was the one who signed all the checks, and as it turned out, he was in a meeting with the elders of the church in Robert's office. I really wanted to get that check signed so I could go about my errands. Robert's secretary said that since they had just started the meeting, it would probably be okay to slip in really quick and get the check signed. I tapped on the door and heard Robert's voice say, "Come in." I said, "Excuse me, could I get a signature really quick before you get started?" Robert motioned in the affirmative and I handed the check to the administrator to sign, which he did. I thanked the men in the room and wished them a good day and stepped out of the office.

Relieved that I had what I needed, I stood by the secretary's desk for a few minutes and chatted with her. The intercom buzzer went off, she pressed the button, and Robert's voice came over the phone speaker. He said (not knowing I was still standing there), "Why did you let him in here during our meeting? Don't ever do that again!"

We looked at each other with that "deer in the headlights" look. I tried not to show any emotion but inside I was crushed. I thought, "I guess that's how he really feels about me." The secretary mouthed the words, "I'm sorry." I laid the check down on the desk and told her to let Robert know that I would not be coming back. At that time, I didn't have the maturity to discern that perhaps they were dealing with some serious confidential matter and didn't want to be interrupted. All I could think of was my own hurt feelings and a sense of rejection.

I drove home and sat on the couch until Margie came home from work. I informed her that we were not going back to RCC. I'm sure she didn't want us to leave, but she supported me in my decision.

I found a new job as a courier out of the airport. This was back in the days when one would drop their photo film off at some retail outlet to be developed. This particular company I worked for collected undeveloped film from stores, transported it to the airport where it would then be shipped out, developed, and returned. I would then deliver the prints back to the original stores.

My route was quite large! It was a route of around 300 miles a day. The company cars we used were small, very compact, and good on gas.

One evening, my little buddy Mark called to check in on me. Somewhere in the conversation he said something about how I ought to forgive Robert and get things right between the two of us. I coldly said, "I'll do that when hell freezes over." Margie heard me say that and she went back in the bedroom to pray, and asked God to do whatever it took to make that situation right. Incidentally, never underestimate the prayers of a godly wife!

The very next day, I had finished my route and was turning left into RDU airport. The light changed and I proceeded into the intersection. Just then, an elderly man driving a full-size Cadillac ran the stoplight and plowed right into my passenger door at about 60 mph. I never saw him coming or remember anything afterward. I woke up in Wake Medical Center with a concussion. I later found out that I had to be cut out of the car with a "Jaws of Life" tool. I had a large contusion on my left shin that had filled up with fluid. I was released and sent home that same evening. I had to be awakened several times that night due to the concussion.

The doctors prescribed two weeks of physical therapy for my neck, which was sore from the accident. After my last therapy session, I went home and fell asleep on the couch. I suddenly woke up to a terrible burning pain in my left shin area where the fluid-filled contusion was. I called Margie at work, and all I could say was, "I need help!"

She rushed home, helped me get in the car, and drove me to the doctor's office. Nurses saw me struggling to get out of the vehicle and came out with a wheelchair. They rolled me in; the doctor assessed the situation and began to drain the injury with a giant syringe. The intense pain subsided and they sent me home with a prescription for antibiotics.

The injury to my leg had contracted a staph infection. The infection did not respond to the antibiotics they gave me, so the doctor increased the dosage. Two weeks later the staph infection was still there and getting worse. The first doctor referred me to a specialist. The specialist was an older Asian man who was very stern. He studied my chart, inspected my injury, and said with insensitive broken English, "We try new antibiotic. If it not work and infection go to bone, we cut off leg."

Those antibiotic pills were about $300 per dose. Fortunately, since this was a worker's comp case, it didn't have to come out of our pocket. I lay in bed at home, praying for God to heal my leg.

The discretion of a man makes him slow to anger,
and his glory is to overlook a transgression.

Proverbs 19:11 NKJV

Chapter 19

The Powerful Antidote

One morning, as I sat in bed watching the TV, unable to do anything else, the PTL Club came on. This was after Jim and Tammy Bakker had left the program. One of the PTL Singers was hosting that day. His name was Ron Aldridge. At one point while he was speaking, he said, "There's someone watching today, and you desperately need a healing in your leg. I believe the Lord is saying, 'If you will forgive the one you feel has wronged you, the Lord will heal you.'" I began to weep as I believed that was a message from God to me. The Bible calls it a "word of knowledge." It is one of the nine gifts of the Spirit mentioned in 1 Corinthians chapters 12 and 14.

I put on a coat and hobbled out to my truck and drove the 15 miles from my house to the church, crying the whole way. I walked into the church's office. No one was sitting at the secretary's desk. I knocked on the door of Robert's office and heard his voice say, "Come in." I hobbled into his office, got down on my knees, and through my sobs told him I was so sorry. He came out from behind his desk and knelt down on the carpet beside me. He embraced me and prayed for me. Our relationship was once again restored. Not only that, but the staph infection in my leg began to leave. Soon it was completely gone, leaving behind a darkened numb area on my shin, which is still there to this day. I think of it as a reminder of what the poison of unforgiveness can do, and to always guard my heart from allowing those toxins into my soul.

Throughout my life up to this point in my story, I had struggled with being offended and harboring unforgiveness toward those whom I believed had mistreated me. This incident broke that stronghold in my life. Now when the offenses come, with the help of the precious Holy Spirit, I forgive quickly and as often as necessary.

I've heard some preachers say, "Unforgiveness is like drinking poison and expecting the other person to die."

So, chosen by God for this new life of love, dress in the wardrobe God picked out for you: compassion, kindness, humility, quiet strength, discipline. Be even-tempered, content with second place, quick to forgive an offense. Forgive as quickly and completely as the Master forgave you. And regardless of what else you put on, wear love. It's your basic, all-purpose garment. Never be without it.

Colossians 3:13-14 (MSG)

Chapter 20

Late Night Buffets

Back in the early days of YouthQuake in Charleston, we had somewhat of a routine. The youth group met on Sunday evenings. On Sunday mornings, Robert Spradley would tell me what he was planning to teach about that night. That would give me a chance to pray and mull it over to determine what song might be appropriate to follow up his message. Often, the Holy Spirit would give me the right song to sing as I walked up to the stage to play. Sometimes not until after I strapped on my guitar and stepped to the microphone. I appreciated the trust and freedom I was given to do that. God was always faithful to "make me to know" what to do.

On one particular Sunday morning, Robert informed me that he was speaking on the subject of loving others like God loves us. He asked if I had any ideas, and I said, "I don't know; let me think about it."

I went home after church that afternoon and wrote a song entitled "Late Night Buffets." I know it sounds like a strange title, but that is what we called our frequent Sunday evening, post-service visits in his kitchen. Diana would go upstairs to put the kids to bed, leaving Robert and me at the kitchen table. We would break out the stainless-steel mixing bowls, milk, and various kinds of cereal. We would chomp and slurp on cereal, and those were times when Robert would often share some awesome insights and what we'd call "nuggets of truth" from God's Word. We would have REAL discussions about life and everything that pertains to it. I could ask questions freely and would always leave enriched. Those were times when real discipleship took place. I treasured them, and really wish we could do them again regularly. Though now it wouldn't be the good stuff, like Cap'n Crunch and Apple Jacks, but probably something high in fiber and tasting like tree bark (sigh).

That night in YouthQuake, I stepped up to the microphone and introduced the song as a tribute to one of the greatest examples of this kind of love I could think of. Here are the lyrics:

Verse 1

"When I see you, all we've gone through, where we've been

You've always been such an example of Him

Through all the years, the laughter and tears

So unselfishly, you put up with me, in spite of my childish fears

Chorus 1

With all those... late night buffets, Cap'n Crunch and Frosted Flakes

And assorted nuggets of truth

My life has been spared, from going nowhere

'Cause you let God love me through you

Verse 2

We've come a long way since that first day that we talked

From a boy to a man, you taught me to stand and to walk

Not just your time, but your life you did impart

And instilled in me, a desire to be, a man after God's own heart

Chorus 2

With all those... late night buffets, Apple Jacks and Special K

And assorted nuggets of truth

My life has been spared, from going nowhere

'Cause you let God love me through you"

© 1991, JEFFERY L STOCKFORD

After the accident and the subsequent restoration, I was privileged to record my first album of all original songs in the Raleigh Christian Community's newly built professional recording studio. Robbie Trice produced it and played acoustic guitar, and Ron Franklin engineered the project and played electric guitar. "Late Night Buffets" was the title track. There was a tremendous array of talented singers and musicians who volunteered their time and talents to make a fantastic album. Tim Hughes played drums, Jon Bass played the fretless bass, Dr. Tim Weir played piano, and Margaret Garris played violin. Some of the singers were Martha Trice, Ernie Frierson, Ginny Franklin, Robin Pope Liner, Jacqui Greggory, Noel and Gay Cookman, and probably a few more.

The whole church got behind the project, and it was a labor of love. It was released in 1991 and I might be a little biased, but I think it still sounds amazing even today!

Oh, sing to the Lord a new song!
Sing to the Lord, all the earth.

Psalm 96:1 NKJV

Chapter 21

Thump-Thump, Thump-Thump

1991 was a year of tremendous blessing in the Stockford household, with restored relationships and the release of my first album. However, another event took place which far overshadowed anything else. It was the birth of our daughter, Grace.

At this point, Margie and I had been married four years and up until then we had not been able to have any children. We didn't get tested or anything but had reached the conclusion that maybe having a child wasn't in God plan for us. Honestly, I think we were both okay with that, but the thought was a bit disappointing.

One evening after eating at our favorite Mongolian Grill restaurant, Margie was feeling a little different. We went to a nearby pharmacy on the way home and picked up a pregnancy test just in case. That evening at home, the test came out positive! We didn't want to get our hopes up too high, though, until it was confirmed by a doctor.

Sure enough, Margie was pregnant! We started preparing as best as we could with our limited financial means at that time. Our friends at church were excited for us though Margie's parents were shocked and didn't know what to think about this news.

The pregnancy progressed fairly normally. I tried to attend all of her OB-GYN appointments so that I could listen to the heartbeat, THUMP-THUMP, THUMP-THUMP... It was music to my ears! Margie got pretty big there for a while. I would describe her as extremely jolly during the latter stages. She even wanted to eat the same kind of food I loved... cheeseburgers and more cheeseburgers, etc. It was like heaven on earth!

One Saturday evening she called me back in the bedroom because she had begun to bleed a lot. We called the emergency OB-GYN number, and they said to come in on Monday. We went through that night and all day Sunday, afraid that she was having a miscarriage and we were going to lose the baby. We held each other a lot during those hours and grieved together. Monday morning came and we headed to the clinic, and to our delight, we heard the blessed sound of THUMP-THUMP, THUMP-THUMP. All was well!

The due date was around Christmas, so we were instructed not to travel for Christmas. We usually went to Margie's parents' house in Wilmington, but that was two hours away. So, we spent a very boring, quiet Christmas at home, watching TV and staring at the walls.

A short time later, Margie thought she was going into labor. We drove to the hospital only to be sent back home, because she wasn't quite ready. We had a nice meal at a local cafeteria and went back home to wait some more. Later that evening her labor started, and there was no mistaking it this time. I rushed her to the hospital, and she was admitted.

Margie was in labor for about 18 hours. As the contractions got more intense and closer together, the team assembled and then she was instructed to start pushing. I watched helplessly as my petite little wife became exhausted. The doctor told her that if she didn't keep pushing, he would have to do a Cesarean section. I witnessed true courage as somehow Margie came up with the strength of will to push more. It worked and our precious daughter, Grace, was born healthy and strong. She didn't do much hollering but glanced around the room with a disturbed look on her little face, as if to say, "Who are all you people?"

Robert and Diana Spradley came to the hospital to visit us. Diana stayed with Margie and the baby in the room while Robert and I headed down to the cafeteria (because we men have to keep up our strength). It had started to sink in, and I began to feel a little overwhelmed at this humongous responsibility God had now entrusted me with. I asked Robert if he thought I would be a good father. He assured me that I would be, and that made me feel better. Our friends Mark and Tammy Shiver also came to see us and to celebrate this momentous occasion! They blessed and encouraged us as well.

When I was a little boy and imagined having my own family, I always only pictured me having one child, and a daughter at that. Grace has been everything I ever dreamed of.

Growing up, Grace (or Gracie, as I used to call her) was my sweet little fun companion. We had a similar sense of humor and spent countless hours making up silly songs and talking in funny voices and accents. We'd do goofy things in public just to see other people's reaction... stuff that would make her mother roll her eyes and pretend not to know us.

As Grace grew older, there was never a problem that two of us couldn't discuss and settle over a milkshake or a 7-Eleven Slurpee. She always loved to drive places with her dad, and we made some precious memories. Grace is now married to a wonderful man, Carsen, and has her own little daughter, Solveig. Grace has a busy life with a successful career. Margie and I are very proud of the woman, wife, and mother she has become.

I have to admit that sometimes I wish I could turn the calendar back to those simple days with my little companion, driving around, making up more goofy songs, stopping for junk food, and being the silly pair we once were. Maybe someday I can have that kind of special, fun relationship with my little granddaughter, too.

Children are a gift from the Lord;
they are a reward from Him.

Psalm 127:3 NLT

Chapter 22

Uncharted Waters

My former church in Charleston, Northwood Assembly, had a vision to help plant new churches. They helped Robert Spradley and his team in planting Raleigh Christian Community (RCC). They were also a big part of planting Seacoast Church in Mount Pleasant, South Carolina, which is now a mega-church with a huge impact nationwide.

One of my dear friends, whom I'll call Tony, was sent out from Northwood Assembly to plant a new church in his hometown, Aiken, South Carolina. This new church became Triple Crown Community Church. A handful of courageous people made the move across the state to be part of Triple Crown's church planting team. I was invited to join them to help with praise and worship and to be Tony's right-hand man.

At that time, I was comfortably leading worship at RCC and enjoying a great time of favor and blessing. I was working for a software company called SAS Institute, which was the best paying job I'd ever had. Margie was working doing accounting for a retirement plan administration business. Grace was now two years old, and we were starting to find some stability.

I agreed to go to Aiken for a one-time visit to lead worship during their first month. They met at a middle school in a multi-purpose room. It was a great service, but I had to tell Tony that I didn't sense that God was leading me to move there. He understood and said to let him know if I ever changed my mind. I'll never forget one of the men, Dave Terry, came up to me with tears in his eyes and asked me to please continue praying about coming. He really felt like I should be part of their team. The fact that he really wanted me touched me deeply, and I've never forgotten that moment.

I returned to Raleigh and continued serving as a volunteer worship leader. Things were going well, but I couldn't get Tony and the church in Aiken off of my mind. About six months later on a Sunday morning, I was in the church office making copies of some chord charts for the musicians when I overheard something that was quite eye-opening. My desire had always been to be in full-time ministry with Robert. But I'd concluded, because of my history and "baggage," it was unlikely to happen again. At times, it seemed like I might be on the brink of being invited to be on staff as the full-time worship leader, but then like a carrot dangling on a stick, it would be pulled away.

As I was in the copy room that morning, not intending to eavesdrop, I overheard someone ask one of the church leaders, "Why don't you guys have Jeff come on staff full-time? He is doing a great job!" This particular church leader laughed out loud and said, "Why would we do that? Why would we pay someone to do something who would do it for free?"

It was in that moment that I realized my desire to be in vocational ministry was never going to happen while at RCC. As discouraging as that was, I felt like God had just released me to go somewhere else. Shortly afterward, I spoke with Tony to see how it was going there in the Aiken church. I mentioned that I was now open to coming to work with him if ever the timing was right.

Not long after that conversation, I got another phone call, and on the other line was Pastor Fred Richard, from Northwood Assembly.

106   I'M TAKING YOU ANOTHER WAY

Tony had informed Pastor Fred that I was open to coming and being a part of the Aiken church team. Pastor Fred proposed that if I would move to Aiken and help with the new fledgling church, Northwood Assembly would make sure I would receive a salary. He even indicated that he thought I could really be a lot of help to them.

Margie and I prayed about it and decided to take a step of faith. I let Robert know what we were planning, and he agreed and released us with his blessing. RCC took up a collection to help us with the move and we received a beautiful plaque of appreciation for our time of ministry there.

The U-Haul truck was loaded, and we drove the four and a half hours to our new home. We found a nice two-bedroom apartment situated on a cul-de-sac. I will never forget how the members of this new little church arrived before us and filled our refrigerator and pantry with good stuff! Dave Terry even went to the hardware store to get components needed to hook up our washer and dryer. I'd never felt so welcomed, valued, and appreciated as I did at that time. Sometimes you have to leave the nest to discover the value you have to others.

I was excited about my first Sunday at Triple Crown Community Church in Aiken. The leadership team gathered in a side room to pray before the service began. Some I knew from my Charleston days, and some had joined in the six months since the church started. I did what I'd always done in those kinds of settings… prayed out loud in English and some in tongues. Right before we went out to start the service, Tony pulled me aside and asked if I would not do that (praying in tongues). I didn't understand why. We'd both come from Pentecostal/Charismatic church backgrounds. This is where I was unknowingly immersed into a church philosophy known as "seeker-sensitive."

I'd been introduced to this philosophy a few years before when the pastor of another church and I were discussing the possibility of me coming to be their worship leader. I didn't end up going there and so I didn't really think much about it after that, until this moment.

I learned that in this type of church, anything that might be misunderstood or controversial was set aside for the sake of unity and reaching the most people possible for Christ. It was pioneered by guys like Bill Hybels and Rick Warren. The intention was noble, which is to remove barriers to someone coming to Christ. Bill Hybels talked about inviting one of his lost friends to church to hear the gospel, and the pastor ended up talking about tithing or some other uncomfortable subject matter that turned his friend off from being a Christian.

I can sympathize with the motivation behind this movement, because as Christians we've been known to do some pretty strange things in church. But I didn't agree with the "seeker-sensitive" approach because I believe the Holy Spirit is the one who draws the lost to Jesus. He is able to do that in spite of our frequent weirdness. However, I also understood spiritual authority and chose to not contradict the pastor I'd committed to serve under.

A few of the members of the leadership team came from more main-line denominations, like Southern Baptist and Presbyterian. They were Cessationist, which means they didn't believe that the gifts of the Holy Spirit, like tongues, prophecy, words of knowledge, etc. are for today. That morning I found myself in a new situation I hadn't been prepared for.

Looking back, I am thankful for being placed in that situation because it caused me to really study to understand not only what I believed, but why I believed it. It also forced me to lock arms with some wonderful godly men who didn't share all my doctrinal beliefs. By God's grace we were able to develop some deep, wonderful relationships, and I respect and value them as my brothers in Christ. I've learned the value of having diversity within the body of Christ. There is much we can all learn from each other!

Behold, how good and how pleasant it is for brethren to dwell together in unity! It is like the precious oil upon the head, running down on the beard, The beard of Aaron, running down on the edge of his garments. It is like the dew of Hermon, descending upon the mountains of Zion; For there the Lord commanded the blessing — Life forevermore.

Psalm 133:1-3 NKJV

Chapter 23

Hard Decisions

I loved working with my friend Tony. The church rented a small office, and I had my own desk and computer. The church seemed to be growing at a good rate. We enjoyed wonderful times of fellowship, collaboration, and laughing a lot. That was what I'd always wanted in a working relationship. Unlike my time with Robert, which was more of a father/son dynamic, Tony and I were like an older and younger brother working together. Our wives got along very well, which was icing on the cake. These were happy times in my memory.

Tony was so good to me. Although I was receiving a salary, he knew it wasn't much, especially with Margie now being a stay-at-home mom. Often, I would go out to my car after the Sunday service and find an anonymously placed envelope with some cash in it on the driver's seat. I know he did it because he loved and cared for me.

I can remember there were a couple of weeks when I would find out at the last minute that I would be giving the message that morning, because Tony wasn't feeling well. That was pretty scary. I usually didn't have anything prepared so I would read through some chapter in the New Testament and make it an expository message. That means I'd read the text and make comments as I went. God was and is faithful, and I can do all things through Christ who gives me strength!

One day, Tony informed me that he and his family were going out of town for a vacation, and they'd be back the next week. He left me in charge of the office and leading the service that coming Sunday. He didn't leave any contact number for me to call if anything happened. This was before the days of cell phones.

The next day while sitting at my desk, the phone rang. It was the principal of the middle school where we'd been meeting. He informed me that they had not been paid their rent in the last three months and if they weren't paid immediately, they would not be unlocking the school for us that Sunday. I told the principal I would find out what happened and get back with him as soon as possible. The next phone call set in motion a chain of events that dramatically changed the lives of everyone involved!

Since I had no way of getting in contact with Tony, I called Northwood Assembly, the home church. I spoke with Pastor Fred and told him what happened. He asked for the contact information for the school and said they would take care of it, but to stay by the phone. A few minutes later, he called back and said that the school had been paid and that we would be able to meet there that Sunday.

Pastor Fred and the Elders of Northwood then came to Aiken to meet with the leadership team and discuss what was going to happen going forward. It was then I learned that Tony had become addicted to pain medication. You see, Tony was a hemophiliac. This condition endangered him in everyday life. Even a bruise could cause him to bleed to death internally. In addition, his ankles had been fused together years before and caused him constant pain. At this time Tony was 36 years old and had outlived many who had the same condition. He'd also been accused of stealing pain medication from someone's medicine cabinet in the church.

Pastor Fred informed me that Tony was being placed on a sabbatical, pending his treatment at an organization known as Emerge, in Akron, Ohio. The program required him to be committed to a psychiatric ward for two weeks for evaluation. Then, he was to receive whatever treatment they prescribed. Tony refused to do the treatment program that required him being locked up for two weeks. Though this refusal greatly concerned Pastor Fred and the Elders, they compromised to allow him to participate in an out-patient program. Another condition was that he couldn't have any contact with the church members for three months, possibly longer.

During this time, I became the interim pastor of the church, with Northwood sending one of their staff pastors to preach twice a month. So, I preached every other week and we'd have what I referred to as "pot-luck pastors" come on the other Sundays.

I learned how to pay the church bills and do the federal and state tax forms for the church's two employees, plus a lot of things I'd always considered "someone else's area." It was like being thrown into the deep end of the pool of church planting, for sure! But I believe that God was in all of it, and He NEVER wastes anything in our growth and development.

On one occasion, I was asked to drive Tony from Aiken to Atlanta, Georgia, about three hours away, for one of his evaluations. It was good to be together again, and it was predetermined that we would not discuss church business. That was all right with me because it would have been awkward. We arrived at the doctor's office, and I left Tony there while I drove up to a Steak-n-Shake restaurant I'd spotted on the drive in... I love that place! I got a big lunch and then drove back to the doctor's office to wait in the lobby for Tony to complete his evaluation.

The waiting room was partially filled, and they had one of those sleep machines in the lobby, making the sounds of ocean waves, probably to calm the patients. I sat back in a chair and decided to close my eyes as a "burger coma" was starting to kick in. Abruptly I was awakened by the sound of a horrifying, deafening roar! It startled me, so I looked around to see what had caused that disruption. Most of the people in the waiting room were glaring angrily at me. The receptionist at the front counter had slid back the glass window and was giving me the same look. It then dawned on me that I had dozed off and had started snoring at an extremely offensive volume. By the way, those noise machines really work. I sheepishly sat up and looked at a magazine, not making further eye-contact with anyone, praying that Tony would come out soon so we could leave.

He finally emerged, and when we started driving back, I told him about what happened. We laughed all the way back to Aiken. When I dropped him off, he said that laugh did him more good than all the counseling and treatments he'd received up to that point. It was like the old Tony was back, which sadly was not true.

The Elders of Northwood didn't like the results of Tony's evaluations and were considering removing him as pastor of the church. However, they decided it would be best if the board of Triple Crown Community Church, which had been put together in the interim, should make the decision whether or not he should be reinstated. That was a difficult meeting, made more stressful because Tony started coming by and lobbying for his return, pressuring some of us to vote him back in. It was an emotional meeting, but we unanimously decided to not allow Tony to continue being the pastor. I remember Rodney, who was Pastor Fred's youngest son, wept over the decision. Tony and his family eventually moved back to Charleston.

I met him for lunch a few years later. He was a broken man, now struggling with addiction to alcohol, but still the gentle, kind man I had known and loved before. He assured me that he held no ill will toward any of us who had decided not to allow him to remain as pastor. But he also chose to reject the many offers to assist him in getting the help he so desperately needed. His marriage later fell apart, and he moved back in with his parents. He eventually died from internal bleeding after a fall in a boating accident. I really miss him and think of him often.

Things continued as they had been, with me speaking every other Sunday and various pastors from the Northwood network of churches coming to fill the other weeks. I led worship and kept the bills paid and up to date.

One of the "pot-luck pastors," whom I'll call Gary, said that he felt the Lord was leading him to come and serve as the lead pastor permanently. Gary, his wife, and two of his kids moved to Aiken after being voted in as the new pastor. He and I got along very well and enjoyed a good working relationship.

One of the first things he did was change the church name to something more generic. The church purchased an abandoned community clubhouse in one of the large neighborhoods. We renovated the large meeting room into a church auditorium and turned the racquetball courts into the children's area with classrooms. There was a large outdoor swimming pool that we had filled in also. It was a big project, but it gave the church a new goal to work towards, putting aside much of the pain of the past. We also saw some families from that neighborhood come to be part of the church and what God was doing there.

As leaders we met together, praying for a move of God to sweep through our church and into the surrounding area. I really wanted to see the church take off, maybe because at this point, I felt like I had so much invested. As the new year came, we as a team were fasting and praying for revival. On the Saturday evening before the first Sunday in January, we had a powerful prayer meeting with great faith and expectation going into the next morning.

Next morning after worship, Gary stepped up to the podium to begin a new teaching series entitled, "New Year - New You." Much to my dismay, the first message was pretty much tips for a healthier lifestyle. My heart sank! I had expected we'd kick off the year with something a little more spiritually focused. I could not believe he would start out the year with something like that. I went home and stewed on it all afternoon. I shared my frustration with a close friend who usually gave me good advice, but this time I'm not so sure. He said that I needed to confront Gary, in love, and tell him what I saw that was wrong.

The next day after making the Monday morning deposit at the bank, I went to drop the receipt off at the church. I saw Gary was there, and asked if we could speak. I proceeded to tell him how I felt about him bringing what I considered a trite message on such an important and pivotal day. At first, he was defensive, so I got a little more forceful in my argument. He started to weep and asked me to pray for him. We knelt down together and prayed, hugged, and then I went home feeling that I had done the Lord's work.

The next morning when I arrived at the office, Gary asked me to step in his office. He told me that I couldn't be the associate pastor there anymore due to insubordination. I basically got fired, but was generously given three months to find another job.

I have to tell you that what I did was WRONG. I should have trusted the Lord to work in that situation. Since then, I heard one teacher say, "The day you can no longer support the pastor's vision is one day past when you should have resigned." Gary didn't deserve my criticism and judging. He deserved my respect and full support. That doesn't mean that two brothers can't disagree and share openly with each other in love. I never bothered to ask him where he was going with this new series of messages. Perhaps he was building up to a subject I was interested in him addressing. Even if not, it was not my place to confront him like that. Looking back, I think spiritual pride played a big role in what I did. I WAS WRONG!

I wish I could say that this was the last time I pulled a bone-headed move like that, but some of us are slow learners. Gary and I are still friends, and he has in later years been a great encourager in my life. I was even invited back to sing at his daughter's wedding.

Likewise you younger people, submit yourselves to your elders.
Yes, all of you be submissive to one another, and be clothed
with humility, for "God resists the proud,
But gives grace to the humble."

1 Peter 5:5 NKJV

Chapter 24

Church Planting is Not for the Faint of Heart

I was determined to make my remaining three months a blessing to Gary. I knew I was in the wrong and didn't want my indiscretion to poison our relationship. We both knew things could not return to the way they were before, but we both decided to part ways demonstrating love and unity.

While I was praying about where my next assignment might be, the thought of Nashville, Tennessee kept coming up. Margie and I decided to take a trip to check it out and prayerfully drive around. At one point we walked around the inside of the Opryland Hotel, which was magnificent! At one end there was a country music trio playing and I could not believe how talented they were. I couldn't understand how this group was not world famous and topping the charts. Then it struck me that this town was full of others that were just as talented, if not more so, doing whatever they could to earn a living. Many were waiting tables, sweeping warehouses or doing whatever they could, while waiting for their big break, which for most never comes.

If we were going to relocate to Nashville, it probably wouldn't be anything having to do with my music. I was way outclassed in that department. It would have to be for something greater than that. Nevertheless, we still felt drawn to move there as an act of faith, to see what God would unfold for us.

I remembered a musician friend of mine who lived there, and thought I'd reconnect with him and see if he had any advice. Years before, he played electric guitar with me in the YouthQuake Band. But now he was an executive at one of the largest Christian record labels in the industry.

After I told him about what we were planning to do, he then proceeded to strongly discourage me from moving there. He spoke of the thousands who move there with stars in their eyes and delusions of grandeur. I'm thinking he didn't want me to come with unrealistic expectations and end up disappointed. He also informed me that my music was "dated."

I felt I had a green light from God to go up to that point, but all of my confidence melted away in about five minutes after speaking to my friend. I didn't see myself as a starry-eyed delusional person, but then I began to question if maybe I really was. To this day, I wonder what would have happened if we'd taken a leap of faith, believed God, and moved to Nashville. But I will never know, because I let someone talk me out of it, and I started looking for another option.

I phoned Robert to see what he thought. He mentioned that a young man in his church at RCC had a desire to plant a new church in Rocky Mount, North Carolina. Robert mentioned that this brother was praying for a team member that could lead worship. Robert also mentioned that perhaps some financial support could be rounded up if we decided to go help him.

Church planting was something I was familiar with, and it sounded like a more secure option than what we were previously considering. So, I drove to Rocky Mount to meet with Richard Gurganus. We had a wonderful day touring the city and imagining what a new church would be like. We decided to move there to help him start a new church. It was to be called Church on the Rise (now known as Rise Church).

The first service happened, and the church was up and running, meeting in a YWCA.

Everything was going well except for one little detail... I didn't have a steady income. The potential support that had been mentioned never materialized, so I started looking for a job. I found one at a large food distributor company, working in the warehouse, pulling orders and unloading trucks. It was back-breaking work.

One day after working there for a few weeks, I was lifting an industrial sized case of green beans. I must have bent over at a weird angle, because suddenly I felt a terrible pain in my back that even made breathing hurt. I went to the manager and told him I was hurt and all he said was that I should probably go to the doctor.

It ended up that I had severely strained my lower back and would need to give it time to heal. I was not able to work for several weeks. Since I was a new employee, they decided to let me go. Here we were, no job, no income, a wife and a young daughter to feed, bills to pay, and no relief in sight. Margie and I both started giving in to despair.

One day a lady in the church came to our door with some bags of groceries. I thought, *Aww, that is so thoughtful and generous.* She smiled and said, "I thought you guys could use a little help, and you know, the Bible says that a man who won't support his own family is worse than an infidel." What she said shocked me and I thought, *Wow, kick a man when he is down, why don't ya, lady!* I'd rather she would have kept the groceries than to give them with that insensitive, judgmental remark.

I eventually found a part-time job at a concrete plant, in the office, adding up yards of concrete. It was a job where I could sit, and the heaviest thing I had to lift was a pencil, but I knew that this situation would not be a long-term solution.

I started searching online at some church staffing websites, looking for something in ministry. Other than ministry stuff, I didn't feel I really had any marketable skills.

I posted my resume and tried to make it look attractive without lying. I was contacted by a pastor in Camden, Arkansas, who flew me out for an interview. I landed in Little Rock, and then was driven the two hours to Camden by the pastor. He was not an overly warm, friendly fellow. He was very formal and distant. That evening I met him at the church as he wanted to hear me rehearse with their praise team. No matter what song I played, they only knew one rhythm, which I refer to as the boom-chick-a-boom bluegrass beat. They even did that rhythm on the slow songs. I can only describe it as what it would sound like if the hillbillies from the movie *Deliverance* decided to start a praise band.

The pastor questioned (more like interrogated) me on several biblical topics. If I didn't answer exactly the way he wanted me to answer, he would say, "WRONG!" like a buzzer on a gameshow. I went back to my hotel room and called Margie and told her I was sorry, but I didn't think this was the place for us. She said that's okay, and by the way, another pastor from Danville, Virginia called, and left a message for you to call him back. I returned his call, and his name was Pastor Tedd Manning. He was the pastor of Cathedral of Praise Church, and he was looking for a worship leader/youth pastor. We agreed to meet after I got back home.

Before leaving Arkansas, I met with the pastor once more for him to show me the parsonage. We walked through a very nice little house close to the church. Then much to my surprise, he asked me if I wanted to accept the position. It took all the self-control I could muster to not yell out, "WRONG!" Instead, I politely declined and thanked him for bringing me there and for considering me to be his worship pastor. Then I flew back to North Carolina and prepared for another interview.

Trust in the Lord with all your heart; do not depend on your own understanding. Seek His will in all you do, and He will show you which path to take.

Proverbs 3:5-6 NLT

Chapter 25

A Genuine Shepherd and a Lifelong Friend

I drove to Danville to meet Pastor Tedd Manning and his wife, Kim. They were a warm, loving, couple who had taken a successful growing church in a desirable area of town and moved it right at the entrance to the Projects in an older, run-down church building. Tedd had a real desire to reach the poor for Jesus. Moving the church across town, to what many considered the bad part of town, cost Tedd a lot of church members and cut the church budget substantially.

In addition, Tedd had to deal with a youth pastor, who had turned many in the church against him. There also were accusations by some in the church that this youth pastor had inappropriate contact with a girl in the youth group. Nothing was ever proven, but he was fired. Tedd and I really connected, and I believed that God wanted us to partner together.

Tedd cared a lot about Margie and me, more than anything I could do for him. He was the kind of person I loved being around! The church finances were very tight, so we both got our paycheck after the Sunday night service offering. Nothing was said, but I know there were times that Tedd sacrificed his paycheck, or some of it, in order to make sure I was paid. I watched him love people most others would reject. Tedd is one of the most Christ-like men I've ever had the privilege to know. Tedd and I spent many happy hours fellowshipping over Chinese or Mexican food.

Pastor Tedd referred to himself as "a black man trapped in a white man's body." He could preach the paint off the walls! Kim was also a gifted preacher! In fact, she had won a national championship when she was on her college debate team. You'd never want to argue with her because even if you were right, she could make you think you were wrong. She was the perfect complement to Tedd.

I led the youth group on Wednesday nights, which was a about 30 kids. Half of them were disinterested, apathetic, white church kids. The other half were African American kids bused in from the Projects. There was not a great deal of interaction, so we took some of our small budget to buy chips, cookies, and soft drinks to have after the teaching. I was amazed at how Margie got in there with those kids and interacted. They liked her, and she made sure each one felt important. She was a big part of that ministry's success. Before we left, the youth ministry tripled and great things were happening amongst the young people. Many young people took on leadership roles and took turns teaching.

The main church services were held in the gymnasium building while the dilapidated sanctuary was being remodeled. One day, Pastor Tedd and I were clearing out some stuff from some unused rooms behind the sanctuary, and we came across a dried, flat carcass of a cat, or a raccoon, or something. We weren't sure. The old building was full of many other surprises as well.

The renovation was a massive undertaking, and Tedd and I were about the most un-handy guys you would ever meet. Other skilled church members would come in to volunteer and supervise and help us with this huge project. We'd often spend a couple of afternoons a week tearing out dry wall or painting. We were about two months from completion, when one day walking through the sanctuary, the

Holy Spirit spoke into my spirit, *"You will not be here when the church moves into this sanctuary."* I wondered why God was moving me; I was very happy there with Tedd. But I didn't say anything to anybody except Margie, and waited to see what would happen.

A friend is always loyal,
and a brother is born to help in time of need.

Proverbs 17:17 NLT

Chapter 26

Yenz Aren't from Around Here

A short time after I sensed the Holy Spirit saying that I would be leaving, I received a call from a pastor from Pittsburgh, Pennsylvania. He had seen my resume that I'd posted online a few years before. He wanted to know if I would be willing to come to Pittsburgh to talk about moving there to help him with a new church plant.

I wasn't wanting to make any changes, but I asked Pastor Tedd what he thought. He strongly encouraged me to go and check it out. He truly wanted what was best for me, even if it meant I would not be able to work with him.

The church in Pittsburgh flew Margie and me up for a weekend, while Grace stayed with her grandparents. Pastor Paul and his wife, Beth, picked us up at the airport and took us to lunch at a Mexican restaurant. When ordering off the menu I asked the waitress for some sweet tea (my favorite beverage). She looked at me kind of perplexed and said, "Yenz aren't from around here, are ya?" They only had unsweetened iced tea with sweetener packets, which doesn't make for sweet tea...sorry, but it doesn't! I found out that nobody up there had sweet tea north of the Mason Dixon Line.

We had a great time of fellowship with Pastor Paul and Beth. The next day I met with another pastor. Pastor Keith was the lead pastor of the "mother church," funding and supporting the church plant I was interviewing for. He was a really nice and godly man who was my age. In many ways he reminded me of Robert Spradley. He had the same air of authority and leadership about him. He explained that I would be working with the mother church part of the week, and then with the new church plant the rest of the time. The new church was going to be meeting in Cranberry Township. It was a very pleasant meeting.

That evening we all met in the large home of one of the families who were part of the new church team. There was a cookout and then we gathered in the living room. Pastor Paul asked me to break out my guitar and lead them in a time of worship. The people who packed out the large room worshipped with great joy and enthusiasm. They were so encouraging to Margie and me. After the worship time, I shared my testimony and then broke into some of my humorous songs, which they loved!

I was offered the position and several of the men in that meeting said that they would rent a truck and come down and move us up there. We found a nice little townhouse for rent and started packing right away. The men came and moved us, and we began a new chapter in Pittsburgh.

We enjoyed a time of great favor with these precious brothers and sisters in Christ. They were some of the most honoring and respectful people we'd ever met. I had, previous to this move, a somewhat negative opinion of northerners as being cold, unkind, and extremely blunt. I found these precious folks to be quite the opposite.

Pastor Paul and some others seemed amused with some of our southern colloquialisms. They would often ask, "Hey Pastor Jeff, what are yenz 'fixin' to do now?"

Pittsburgh can get very cold, at least to a Florida boy. It was a bitter, cold winter, and I can remember preparing to step outside, looking at the thermometer and seeing that it was 19 degrees. I thought, *Oh great! It's finally starting to warm up!*

The church met in an elementary school. The school graciously let us store our equipment in a closet in the auditorium where we met. Later the church was able to purchase some property to build a permanent home. As great as things were going along with wonderful relationships, this chapter ended after about eighteen months. Sadly, I was the one who sabotaged it.

One evening the leaders met to resolve some growing tension between Pastor Paul and me. Most of it had to do with the possibility of me having to take a significant pay cut in order to finalize the building on the new property. I felt that was unfair because there was no mention of it applying to him as well. It appeared to me that he really didn't care about my family's well-being. Things got heated and in anger, I lashed out at Paul and said something derogatory. One of the brothers, a precious Indian man said, "Oh no, brothers, we must not speak like this!" I immediately felt ashamed for giving voice to that impulse.

That anger issue, when pushed to a certain point, was still present in my life. Once again it not only cost me my job but also ruined my reputation with some people whom I cared about.

I was given two weeks and the church gave us a going away reception after my last service. One year later, I returned to play in a wedding of one of my much-loved friends and former praise team members, Debra Erskine. I made it a point to meet with Paul and once again apologized for being disrespectful. He was gracious and assured me that he had forgiven me right away.

Those who control their tongue will have a long life; opening your mouth can ruin everything.

Proverbs 13:3 NLT

Chapter 27

A Game Changer

I want to tell you about something else that happened about midway through my time in Pittsburgh. I was introduced to a revelation of God's amazing grace toward me. It happened on a dark, lonely Christmas Eve drive as I was traveling from Pittsburgh, PA to Wilmington, NC. I was driving to join Margie and Grace at Margie's parents' house for Christmas. The church where I was serving as worship pastor had a Christmas Eve service which I had to be there for. Margie and Grace had traveled to Wilmington by train about a week earlier. The plan was for me to make the 10-hour drive as soon as the service was over.

I was weary and exhausted, physically and emotionally, at that point. Out of boredom, I popped in a cassette tape that my buddy Mark Shiver had given me almost a year earlier. It was a teaching by an Orlando based attorney named James Barron. James had received a powerful revelation of the finished work of Christ on the cross and God's amazing grace. It radically transformed his spiritual paradigm. As I listened, he addressed things that were commonly taught in churches that are not true. He spoke with passion and authority and his knowledge of the Scriptures held my attention.

This teaching was unlike anything I'd ever heard. At first, I thought this sounded too good to be true (what kind of a weird cult is my buddy Mark into?). Then, unexpectedly, tears began to roll down my cheeks as I found myself wishing James' teaching about God's amazing grace was true. A few days later, I contacted James, and we began corresponding by email. He patiently allowed me to ask questions, raise objections, and try to poke holes in his teaching. For me this was too important to get wrong; I had to know the truth! He answered each question with a lengthy, loving, thoughtful answer. After several weeks of back and forth, it was like a light bulb came on in my mind. I became convinced that the Gospel, which means "good news," is really a lot better news than I'd imagined! James always ended his emails with, "I love you, bud!" Those words touched my heart as well.

I began to see the Bible through a different lens. The best way to describe it is like when you go to a 3-D movie and they give you special glasses. Looking at the screen without them, I could see images, but they were blurry and not very well defined. However, when I put the 3-D glasses on, the images didn't just come into focus, they seemed to jump right off the screen. It was like I could reach out my hand and touch them. That is what the Word of God became for me, and I couldn't get enough! I began to see the importance of rightly interpreting the Scriptures, recognizing which covenant applies to what is being read, along with the correct context.

I'd spent a good part of my Christian journey with a constant sin-consciousness mentality, kind of like a hamster running on a wheel, falling off, getting back on, then falling off again. I was trying to maintain a pure and holy life but constantly failing and feeling God was very disappointed in me, maybe even disgusted. So often I felt like a phony. My entire view of how God felt about me was based on how well I performed my "Christian To-Do List." This made for a non-victorious, insecure version of Christianity. I was probably projecting onto God some of the emotional scars of my upbringing. God used James' teaching, along with our interactions and friendship, to forever alter my perception of how God sees His children. I started becoming established in God's unchanging love and got off the "hamster wheel." I still do the things on the "Christian To-Do List," not to get God's favor, but because I have it already. Living FROM God's favor instead living to GET God's favor makes a world of difference!

Many devoted Christians have a hard time accepting that Jesus ran our race perfectly, then took His righteousness (right-standing with His Father) and bestowed it on us. It is completely unearned and is given as a gift. This runs contrary to what is commonly taught in many churches today. There just seems to be something in our flesh that wants to contribute to our right standing with God. But the truth is, we add nothing, it is 100% Jesus, no added ingredients! Our part is to simply believe. Seeing life through the lens of grace doesn't make light of sin, but it does make much of Jesus and His sacrifice for sin. We who are born-again have been given the very righteousness of Jesus Himself. This amazing gift doesn't make me want to run out and sin and see how far I can push the limits of His grace. It makes me want to live a holy life that reflects and honors my wonderful Savior!

This wonderful truth of the Gospel of Grace has been one of the biggest "game changers" in my life! It has caused a little persecution from some who didn't understand, but I can never go back to the way it was. It's exciting to see that many around the world are experiencing the same awakening that I have. I owe James Barron a huge debt of gratitude. He has become one of my dearest friends and continues to encourage and cheer me on. You can find many of his messages on seeinggrace.com.

For He made Him who knew no sin to be sin for us, that we might become the righteousness of God in Him.

2 Corinthians 5:21 NKJV

Chapter 28

A Strange Assignment

After leaving Pennsylvania we moved back to good ol' North Carolina where they know something about how to make sweet tea. We ended up being invited to help with another church plant in Wake Forest, a small town north of Raleigh. For the first time Margie and I were able to purchase our own house. It was brand new and a dream home, especially to Margie.

At first, the pastor and I shared great comradery. The church met in an older hotel and the church office was in the pastor's home basement. We had some wonderful times, and I made some dear friends that are still very special to me today.

Eventually the meeting location had to change, as the hotel was sold and going to be demolished. We rented a banquet room in a local restaurant while a new church building was being built on some purchased property.

Things went "south" after one particular leaders' meeting. At this meeting, the pastor was very harsh and unreasonable, speaking to one of the men in the meeting. This particular man was a very devoted volunteer in the church. Driving home with the pastor afterward, he asked me what I thought of his confrontation with that leader. I said (very respectfully), "I thought that maybe you were a little harsh with the brother." The pastor got kind of quiet after that, and I could tell what I said wasn't what he wanted to hear. This was my first clue that my situation might be headed in the wrong direction.

A few weeks later, Pastor Fred from Northwood Church contacted me to see if I was available to come to Charleston on a Wednesday night to lead a night of worship. We currently weren't having meetings on Wednesday nights, and I'd earned some vacation time, so I brought it up with the pastor the next morning. When I asked for the time off, he looked at me rather coldly and said, "We're really not talking about time off, we're talking about transition." He then proceeded to tell me that I would no longer be working for that church.

This took me by complete surprise, but I calmly replied, "Okay, I understand." He said that the church would pay me for one month, and during that time I would lead worship every Sunday, and unlock the nearly finished church facility for the contractors, every morning at 7:00 am and lock it back up at 6:00 pm.

I knew I had done nothing that deserved termination this time. I believe that when he asked my opinion about that confrontation with the other church leader, he interpreted my response as disloyalty. But, in a way, I was relieved, because I'd seen some questionable practices by this pastor. He took advantage of some of the church members, feeling entitled to receiving free gifts and personal services from them.

The following Sunday, I said nothing to the other musicians and leaders. I went to the banquet room, set up, and led worship as usual. At the end of the pastor's message, I slipped up quietly and began to play my guitar softly as he gave the salvation challenge. After that, he said that he had an announcement to make. It went something like this, "Pastor Jeff and Margie no longer want to be part of our church, so they have been released and today is their final Sunday." There was no staying until the end of the month as I was informed earlier. It certainly was not my idea to leave. The congregation was surprised and some gasped and whispered, "No!"

By the way, I was still up in front of everybody, playing softly on my guitar. I felt the Holy Spirit sternly warn me, *"Do not defend yourself, don't even make any facial expressions that would indicate disagreement with what the pastor said, even though he lied to the people. Even the slightest gesture might split this church apart, and I do not want you to do that. I will take care of you."*

By God's grace I kept a calm demeanor and that completed my eleven-month stint at that church. God saw this coming and prepared another open door for us.

I have forgiven this brother for what he did, and I only write of this because it was pivotal in getting me to the next stop on my strange zig-zaggy, circuitous journey.

Make allowance for each other's faults, and forgive anyone who offends you. Remember, the Lord forgave you, so you must forgive others.

Colossians 3:13 NLT

Chapter 29

The Man with a Kind Voice

I received an invitation to try out to be the worship pastor for a new Anglican-Pentecostal church in Raleigh. While preparing for the upcoming service, my daughter Grace, who was seven or eight years old at this time, said something absolutely amazing!

She said, "Dad, the church you are playing at this Sunday is not the one that the Lord wants us to go to. And so that you will know that this is true, the pastor will preach from the book of John, chapter six."

I was dumbfounded! Who is this little blonde-haired prophetess living under my roof? Then I said, "Be quiet, sweetie, Daddy needs a job!"

She went back to her bedroom and came out a few minutes later and said, "By the way, in two weeks you will receive a phone call from a man with a kind voice. He is the one you are to go to work with." Who says that God can't use little children?

That morning we went to this church in Raleigh. It was a little strange, because they were more liturgical than anything I was familiar with. They also used real wine for communion, so our family passed on that and only ate the bread. I led some familiar worship songs and the pastor stepped up to speak. He said, "Our text this morning comes from the Gospel of John, chapter six..." I looked over at my daughter Grace, and she looked at me with the smuggest, I-told-you-so face I'd ever seen. We finished the service and drove straight to Myrtle Beach, South Carolina for a little R&R.

A few weeks later I was sitting in the living room and the phone rang. Grace ran to answer it saying, "Hello, Stockford residence... yes, he is, I'll go get him." She came to me and said, "Dad it's for you, it's the man with a kind voice." My jaw dropped open and I went to the back room to find out who this was on the other end of the phone.

The man with a kind voice was a dear friend, Greg Wigfield. He was one of Robert Spradley's closest friends, and so he became mine by extension. We'd spent some great times together over the years. He lived in Leesburg, Virginia, about 30 minutes outside of Washington D.C. He was a successful businessman, an incredible musician/singer, and was the chaplain for the Washington Redskins during the Joe Gibbs years. A few years before that phone call, Greg had felt called to start a church, called Destiny Church, and it had been growing and seeing tremendous blessings.

Greg asked what I was doing, then asked if I'd be open to coming to Leesburg and leading worship and serving as his associate pastor. We prayed and felt God saying to go. I moved up first, and Margie and Grace stayed behind to sell our house in Wake Forest. We enjoyed being around Greg and Pam. He was so easy to talk to and encouraging. One thing that may have seemed like a small thing, but was a huge thing to me, was that up to this point, many of my prior church ministry positions came with fairly meager pay and zero insurance benefits. Most of the churches couldn't afford them. Greg made sure we were well paid, and when he said that my salary included health insurance, it brought me to tears.

One of the things I took on, working with Greg, was all the printed media and the website. I learned a lot of new things and my skillset grew by leaps and bounds. He introduced me to the world of Apple/Mac, and I've never looked back.

Those were happy times for our entire family, and I will always be thankful to God for sending me to work with "the man with a kind voice." On one occasion, Greg, some other church leaders, and I attended a church leadership conference. Greg saw to it that all our expenses were paid, and even sprung for all the meals and snacks on the trip. He and his sweet wife, Pam, genuinely cared about us.

On Father's Day one year, Greg asked me to share a tribute to my earthly father. I told him that wasn't a good idea as the relationship with my father was practically non-existent. He said, "The very least you could do is thank God for the fact that because of him you have life. Furthermore, because you have life you were able to come to know Jesus." He had a point there, so I did what he asked. I publicly thanked God for my father even though I barely knew him. I didn't realize at the time what was going to follow.

Shortly after that, I received an unexpected call from my brother Kalvin (who had never called me before) informing me that our father was in the hospital and not expected to live much longer. He said that if I wanted to see him before he died, I should come now.

I mentioned that to Greg but had no intention of going to Florida to see him. I wasn't bitter, just indifferent. Greg insisted that I fly down and he paid for the plane tickets for Grace and me to go, including a rental car, meals, and a hotel. Greg has always been extremely generous.

We flew down and walked into the hospital room to see my father looking emaciated and very frail. We had a pleasant conversation and he seemed thrilled to see me and to meet his granddaughter, Grace. As we spoke, I began to realize much of what I had believed about him, and how he felt about me was inaccurate, tainted by my mother's bitterness. I came back home with a new perspective on some of the events of my life after that. I'll share more in the next chapter.

JEFFERY L. STOCKFORD

A couple of months later, my brother Kalvin called again and somewhere in the course of the conversation, he casually mentioned that he had become a Christian. That news was the shock of a lifetime! Kalvin was the last person on the planet that I would ever imagine becoming a Christian! That proves that nobody is beyond God's reach!

Kalvin was a foreman for a tree service and went to collect on a recent job they had completed. The customer was a lady bodybuilder who had prayed that morning, saying, "Lord, whoever You send to me today, I will tell them about You." Then, a large man with a long gray beard and a booming voice came to her door. She did what she promised the Lord and ended up leading my brother Kalvin in the sinner's prayer. Kalvin began attending my old church, Calvary Assembly, and became part of the singles ministry. He would come early and make the coffee for everyone. One year he even dressed up as Santa Claus for the single parents' kids. This was nothing short of an absolute miracle!!!

Back to Leesburg, Virginia, and Destiny Church... around that time, Greg and I attended a week-long conference in Dallas, Texas. It had something to do with taking your church to the next level. Greg was always an innovator with an eye to the future. At this conference, the worship was very dynamic, exciting, and it was obvious that a lot of planning went into it. I've always been one of those more spontaneous flow-and-go in the Spirit types. To do what they were demonstrating at this conference, though very inspirational, was somewhat outside of the way I was wired.

However, it became clear that this was the direction Greg felt the church should go, and even more clear that it was not something in which I could help lead the church (with my present paradigm). We decided that it was best if I moved aside. It was difficult and painful but necessary. Looking back, there are things I would have handled differently, but this was the right decision for Destiny Church, and for our family.

I love Greg and Pam very much and will always treasure his friendship. I look forward to any time I get to spend with him!

To everything there is a season, a time for every purpose under heaven: a time to be born, and a time to die; a time to plant, and a time to pluck what is planted;

Ecclesiastes 3:1-2 NKJV

Chapter 30

"My Masterpiece"

Greg recommended that I meet with the director of a large church-planting organization located in Charleston, South Carolina. Perhaps he would know of a ministry situation that might be a good fit for me. I called and the director seemed happy to meet with me, so an appointment was made for the following week.

I drove down to Charleston very hopeful of what the Lord might have for me next. I was tired of church planting, but it was an area I had a lot of experience in. I was willing to give it another shot.

I arrived at the office and waited to be called back to meet with this man. I'd heard him speak before at a conference I had attended with Greg. At that time, I had been so impressed with how loving and kind he seemed as he spoke. I knew in my heart this would be a good and productive meeting.

He came to the lobby and led me back to his office. He entered before me, sat behind his desk, and asked me to close the door. I did, and he confirmed what our appointment was about. "So, tell me, what are you looking for as far as a ministry position goes?"

I replied, "I'm open to just about anything, but my best skills and experience are primarily in the area of leading praise and worship and church planting."

His face got really serious and then he said something I would have never expected him to say. He said, "You're fat! What makes you think that any pastor would want to put someone who looks like you up on the platform before their people?"

OUCH! That hurt! I was taken aback to say the least. I went from feeling hopeful to feeling very ashamed. I pretty much didn't hear anything he had to say after that. I'm a big guy and have struggled with my weight most of my adult life. But I never considered myself so horrible looking as to make a potential pastor ashamed to show me in public.

The meeting ended and I drove to a parking lot and called Margie to tell her what happened. She said, "It's okay, God has something for us, just come back home." It was a long, quiet drive back to Leesburg, Virginia. No radio or CD's playing, just me alone with my thoughts. Have you ever felt too discouraged to even pray? I did. Up until then I'd only wanted to serve in ministry, but now it didn't seem very desirable at all.

Our townhouse went on the market, and it went under contract after one day. We had to move somewhere. I looked for jobs online, anything but ministry, because at this point, I was burned out and done with vocational ministry. But the only job opening I found that looked like it would potentially work out was in Orlando, at my old home church, Calvary Assembly. It was a non-ministry position as a graphic designer, doing bulletins, newsletters, flyers, etc. My friend Chip, one of the guys from my old basketball team, now served on the pastoral staff there. I asked him if I could use him as a reference and also if he would put in a good word for me. He said he would.

I got an interview with the executive pastor hiring for the position, so I drove about 15 hours to meet with him at the church the next morning. I came to his office for my interview only to find out that he got invited to play in a golf tournament and wasn't going to be there. I left the church feeling extremely discouraged, especially after having driven all that way.

I stopped in to visit with my father, who was very frail and living in a small travel trailer with my brother Kalvin. We spoke for a few minutes, then I started the long journey back to Virginia. I got about an hour outside of Orlando, and the voice of the Lord spoke to me once again, loud and clear. It was unmistakable. He said, *"Turn around and go get an apartment!"*

I pulled over and phoned Margie to tell her what the Lord had said. She replied, "You do what you believe He wants you to do, I'm with you!" So, I turned around and went back to Orlando and secured an apartment. Then I headed back to Virginia and we started packing to move.

We made the move with the help of some new South African friends who were planning to visit Walt Disney World anyway. They were truly a gift from God! After they helped us get moved in, they went to Disney and took Grace with them.

I once again returned to Calvary Assembly to interview with the executive pastor. I showed him some samples of my work, and he said to call him back in a couple of days. I walked out into the church parking lot and looked up to the sky and prayed out loud, "God! Give me this job!" I wasn't used to praying bold prayers like that, but I believe that is something God may want us to do more of.

I followed up with the executive pastor, and he invited me to come back in. He said to me, "I was a little underwhelmed at your samples."

Then I said, "How about this: why don't you let me work for you, for free, for two weeks? If after that you don't like what I do, I'll move on, but at least you'll have the work covered."

He said, "You know, there's something about you, so I'm going to take a chance on you. We'll hire you on a contract basis." That basically meant I got paid, but with no benefits. I accepted the job.

I went there hoping to get away from being in the ministry. But over time, the gifts and calling of God began to become evident. I was asked to lead worship for various kinds of meetings, and to play guitar in the orchestra on Sunday mornings. My favorite times were leading worship for the Son-Lighters, Calvary's seniors ministry. Pastor Mike Martin, who led the seniors ministry, and I became good friends. I continued to do Calvary's graphic design, and everyone on the large staff was extremely kind and encouraging.

I made it a point to visit my father every few days or so. At this point he had pretty much stopped eating, so I would buy him some Ensure drinks, to give him a little nutrition. One day I mentioned that it was wonderful to learn that the father I thought didn't care about me really wanted to be in my life. His reply floored me! He said, "Jeff, I've always thought of you as being my masterpiece." I can't begin to express how much that meant to me. God has blessed me with several amazing "spiritual fathers," but to hear those words from my real earthly father began to heal a lifetime of deep wounds that even today I don't fully understand. Something in me changed that day.

Margie and I did what we could for him, but he passed away one night in his sleep about two months after we moved to Florida. I'd asked him shortly before that if he was ready to go to meet Jesus. He assured me that he was. I had the honor of officiating his funeral. How amazing that God would orchestrate the circumstances of my life to be with him for those final months, and to hear the things a son should hear from his father. Thank You, Jesus!

Maybe people in your life have criticized you and made you feel as if you have little or no value. Maybe someone has said to you, "You're fat, or ugly, or stupid, or a loser..." Don't listen to those voices playing over and over in your mind. Instead, every time you feel worthless, imagine your Heavenly Father saying to you, "I've always thought of you as My masterpiece!"

I praise You, for I am awesomely, wonderfully made!
Wonderful are Your works—
and my soul knows that very well.

Psalm 139:14 TLV

Chapter 31

Help! I Think My Mom Married an Assassin!

My mother had remarried a man whom I'll call Emmitt. It was an unusual match, to say the least! She met him through a classified ad, the same way she had met her previous husband, Carl. They dated for a week or so, then he moved her and my aging Great Aunt Beth up to be with him in Metter, Georgia.

Previously, while we were living in Wake Forest, my mom and Emmitt had come to visit us, and Emmitt spoke about how he had done spy work for Oliver North and had been an assassin for the government. He said he'd made a provision in his will to give each of my mother's kids one million dollars when he died. I thought to myself, *I'll believe that when I see it.* I think he was saying that to impress my mom. Incidentally, that check never arrived.

One time Margie, Grace and I went to visit them in Metter. It was a shock to our system. I don't even know how to adequately describe what we experienced. We arrived and sat down at their dinner table, and immediately began to see cockroaches running across the table. They were on the walls, the refrigerator, falling off the light fixtures onto the food. There were even roaches in the Jell-O. Nobody said anything. My mother and Emmitt carried on as if nothing was out of the ordinary.

What do you do? What do you say about something like that? We retired to a small bedroom that they had prepared for us, with one bed for Margie and me, and a small child's mattress on the floor for Grace. By this time Grace was a teenager so she slept in a chair. That night before we turned off the lights, the three of us prayed that God would keep the roaches and spiders away from us. And God did exactly that!

Emmitt was a man who lived a double life. In town he was known as a businessman. In reality, according to his story, he had worked for the CIA under George H.W. Bush and was an assassin. He showed me four or five sniper rifles he pulled from under his bed. They were not your typical 30-30 or 30-06 guns, they were AR-50s and Barrett M-99s, meant to hit a target from a very long distance. He showed me bullet hole scars in his leg. He told me of escaping from a prison in Central America. He said that he was always expecting the government to send someone to take him out one day. He had many loaded guns located throughout his house within arm's reach.

Emmitt owned a large piece of property with pecan trees and about four warehouses. They were filled with things he would buy whenever he got the notion. If gas generators were on sale at Home Depot, he wouldn't only buy one, he'd buy ten. The warehouses were filled with almost anything you would need or want, along with a bunch of junk. I don't know what he was planning to do with all that stuff, but he could have opened his own store.

I think that my mother may have been living in fear of him. She would never speak for herself, and if I asked her anything, she would always tell me to talk to Emmitt.

That visit was one of the most bizarre experiences of my life. I can't believe that Margie and Grace were able to hold it together with all the roaches there. It seemed like some kind of insanity to live that way while acting like it was normal.

We three were so grossed out by the multitude of roaches everywhere, even on the refrigerator door handles, that we claimed to not be very hungry and declined breakfast the next morning. We left the following day after I played a couple of songs at the church they attended. We stopped at the first restaurant we came to, which was a Ryan's Steakhouse. We ate like a pack of crazed, starving wolves and stuffed ourselves. I thanked Margie and Grace for the self-control and graciousness they had demonstrated and promised that I wouldn't put them through something like that again.

One afternoon I got a call from Kalvin that my mother had a stroke and was in a hospital in Savannah, Georgia. I drove up and waited most of the night to see her. She was in the ICU. My brother and some of Emmitt's relatives were there as well. When I was finally allowed to come back and see her, she was awake and had been given a breathing tube. I leaned over her and said, "Hi mom, I'm here." She looked at me with a panicked look, and kept mouthing, "I CAN'T BREATHE!" I tried to get her to relax, but she was in great distress. I said to the nurse, "She says she can't breathe." The nurse assured me that she could, but that she was fighting the respirator. They were getting ready to sedate her, so I left the room. That was the last time I saw her alive. We didn't get to have any kind of meaningful conversation. She passed away in the hospital.

She and Emmitt had attended the Church of God, in Metter. I spoke and sang at her funeral. Before the service began, I saw Emmitt slumped over a car in the parking lot. I went to check on him and he began to weep profusely. I physically held him up because he seemed as if he was about to collapse. I assured him that he was going to get through this. He was able to compose himself and returned to the church sanctuary.

All of my mom's possessions, including her car, were promised to me, to distribute to the rest of her children. I never saw anything of hers, as Emmitt and his family kept it all. Emmitt passed away a few months later, and I returned to Metter one last time to take part in his funeral service, to pay my respects. A few years later I learned that

Emmitt forged my mother's signature on some of her life insurance policies in order to defraud my siblings and me of the proceeds. Good thing my Heavenly Father is my source who supplies all my needs according to His riches and glory by Christ Jesus.

> [2] *Dear brothers and sisters, when troubles of any kind come your way, consider it an opportunity for great joy.*
> [3] *For you know that when your faith is tested, your endurance has a chance to grow.* [4] *So let it grow, for when your endurance is fully developed, you will be perfect and complete, needing nothing.*

James 1:2-4 NLT

Chapter 32

Training Unaware

Calvary Assembly had a change in pastoral leadership. A new senior pastor came to lead the church. His name was George Cope. He was the former president of Zion Bible College, and we got along very well. My favorite part of the work week was on Mondays. Shortly after I arrived at the office, he would call and say, "Come on down!" I would come to his office, and we would collaborate on his next sermon. We'd bounce creative ideas off one another, and research the Scriptures and potential sermon illustrations. I'd give him ideas on how to package the sermon or sermon series. It was very enjoyable! What I didn't realize at the time was that Pastor George was helping me to develop the ability do something I didn't think I could do, coming up with weekly sermons. This was a skill that I would draw upon later.

One afternoon as I was having lunch in my car, out of the blue, the Lord spoke to me again in His unmistakable voice, saying, *"I want you to transfer your ministerial credentials to the Assemblies of God."* I had previously received my ordination with an organization Robert Spradley had established, called World Changers International. Later it became Destiny Fellowship.

Through a series of events that only God could have orchestrated, I was able to transfer my credentials, after some online courses and passing a five-hour test. On May 6, 2006, I was honored to participate in a formal ordination service. The minister who was assigned to lay hands on me was the legendary Pastor Dan Betzer.

Shortly after that event, I was promoted and was brought onto the pastoral staff as one of thirteen pastors. I was put in charge of pastoral care/hospital visitation/visitor follow-up and pretty much all the other stuff that none of the others wanted to do. I turned over all the graphic design responsibilities and website development to some very talented people so that I could concentrate on ministry responsibilities.

During my time as a graphic designer, I became very close to several on the support staff at the church who worked in maintenance, grounds-keeping, security, custodial, etc. We would all often go to lunch together at various restaurants in the area. We had so many good times and laughs. I will tell you that there were some real "characters" in that group! After coming onto the pastoral team, I continued to go to lunch with those guys, though most of the other pastors fellowshipped amongst themselves. I really miss those times.

I didn't realize it at the time, but God was skillfully preparing me for the future. Someone once said, God doesn't cause everything that happens, but He never wastes anything either. He often intersects our lives with what seems like random people. Often those encounters are what He uses to make an important deposit in our life, character, and destiny.

For I know the thoughts that I think toward you, says the Lord, thoughts of peace and not of evil, to give you a future and a hope.

Jeremiah 29:11 NKJV

Chapter 33

Crime Scene

On Monday morning, July 9, 2007, I came into the office and got a phone call from Bill Gray, the church administrator. He and some of the maintenance guys had come back from breakfast and saw crime-scene tape around the Gator Tree Service office, where my brother Kalvin both worked and lived. He called me to say I should go down there to check and see if Kalvin was all right. The tree service office was only a block over from the church campus. I walked over and stepped under the crime-scene tape and told the police officer that my brother lived there.

I was informed that my brother was found dead and was then questioned by a lady police officer and was asked to remain there outside in case they needed additional information.

I spoke to the co-worker who had come in and discovered his body lying right inside the doorway. He said that previously Kalvin had won $10,000 playing the lottery. Kalvin had boasted about it to some of his co-workers. Since Kalvin didn't have a bank account, he kept his money in his boot, which most of his crew knew.

Here is what transpired as I understand it. Kalvin came home from the singles Bible study on Sunday evening. Shortly after he arrived, he received a knock at the door. As soon as he opened it, Dwayne

Ricardo Smith, a co-worker with a history of violent crimes, shot him in the head twice with a stolen handgun. He robbed him, then ran outside to a waiting driver.

They went to nearby Lake Fairview and disposed of the gun and the box of bullets. Smith's friend who drove the car, was later questioned, and told detectives about a night that began with murder and ended with strippers, drinks, and lap dances. Dwayne Ricardo Smith was arrested two days later and charged with first-degree murder and held without bond in the Orange County Jail.

The funeral was unbelievable! I was shocked that more than 200 people from all walks of life came into the chapel. Many stood up to speak of their affection and appreciation for Kalvin. His boss stood up and talked about how Kalvin had become a devout Christian and really turned his life around. It was touching to see how my burly, rough brother had touched so many lives.

I officiated the service with the help of Pastor George Cope and some of the church staff members. Following the service something else happened that forever transformed my perspective.

Kalvin's co-workers were very different from the kind of people I had ever associated with. They were what I would describe as rough, tough, tattooed, hard living people. It would seem that I would have very little in common with them and we'd probably avoid each other in most circumstances. But this day, they decided to celebrate Kalvin's life with a picnic in a park by the lake. They had a meal catered by Kalvin's favorite BBQ place and invited Margie, Grace, and me to join them.

For a few hours, us three prim, proper, strait-laced, church folks were loved on, honored, and comforted by these precious people. All judgement was suspended as we found acceptance and genuine care in the most unexpected environment.

In a period of eighteen months, I buried my father, mother, stepfather, and brother. Each was impactful in its own way. It felt as though I was also burying a big part of my past.

...whereas you do not know what will happen tomorrow. For what is your life? It is even a vapor that appears for a little time and then vanishes away.

James 4:14 NKJV

So teach us to number our days,
That we may gain a heart of wisdom.

Psalm 90:12 NKJV

Chapter 34

What's a Guy Like Me Doing in a Place Like This?

Later I received an invitation to meet with the Orange County Assistant District Attorney, a tall young woman named Erin. She wanted to discuss what they were planning for the case against Dwayne Ricardo Smith. She asked me to be part of every phase of the upcoming trial, from jury selection to verdict and sentencing. She informed me that they were not going to seek the death penalty but a life sentence without the chance of parole. She felt that they had a better chance of getting a conviction that way. I told her to do what she believed would be best.

The trial date arrived, and I showed up for jury selection and sat on the back row of the gallery with the jury candidates. The attorneys entered with the defendant, accompanied by two sheriff's deputies. The lawyers and defendant were seated facing the jury pool. Then Judge Belvin Perry entered, the same judge who would preside over the Casey Anthony trial one year later. We arose and then he gave the jury candidates instructions.

Seeing the defendant was a surreal experience. He was a very dark-skinned African American, wearing a badly fitting white dress shirt and gray dress pants. He looked so evil, glaring at the jury candidates while they were being questioned. Throughout the day the pool of jurors thinned out as I remained on the back row. At one point when there was nobody sitting in front of me, he looked directly at me with a hateful look. I assume he recognized the similarity between my brother and me, minus the long hair and Santa beard. He must have figured out that I was Kalvin's brother. Maybe I was overly sensitive, but the old saying, "If looks could kill..." would have applied here.

The jury was selected that Monday afternoon, and the trial was to begin the next morning. The judge mentioned that he expected all the proceedings to be wrapped up by the end of the day on Friday. That week the testimony went back and forth. The state had powerful evidence. They had recovered the box of bullets and used the barcode to track where they were purchased. They had video of the driver of the car buying the bullets at a Walmart. They had his testimony as well as the testimony of the defendant's girlfriend, who was now also an inmate.

Dr. Jan Garavaglia from the popular TV show *Dr. G: Medical Examiner* was the actual coroner who examined Kalvin's body and testified in court one day.

The prosecution's case seemed very solid. However, the defense's case was based on making my brother out to be an evil, hate-filled racist. By the time the defense attorney was finished presenting his case, I began to be concerned that this case might go the other way. I didn't imagine at that time that lawyers were allowed to say anything even if it wasn't true, to save their client. I naively thought they had to stay somewhat within the parameters of the truth.

After the proceedings on Wednesday, I found myself riding down the elevator with the defense attorney. He looked at me apologetically and said, "I'm sorry about all that, but I'm only doing my job for my client."

I thanked him and said, "I understand. I want you to do the best job you can so that this case doesn't get messed up in some way." The elevator reached the ground floor, and we wished each other a good evening.

Closing arguments were the next morning, which included some gruesome photos of my brother's injuries. The judge, attorneys, and jury members looked at the screen, and then I noticed all their eyes staring at me to see if I would react. I remained stoic and didn't make eye contact with anyone.

The Assistant District Attorney wrapped up the prosecution's case in what I can only describe as a slam dunk! She masterfully brought out the facts of the case, adding each one of them as spokes of a wheel on a big drawing board in front of the jury box. The case was then handed over to the jury to deliberate.

As I left the court on that Thursday afternoon, I ended up on the elevator with a petite little African American lady who had been sitting quietly in the back of the courtroom all week on the opposite side from where I sat. She looked up at me and asked, "You are his brother, aren't you?"

I said, "Yes ma'am."

She said, "I'm Dwayne's stepmother and I am so sorry!" She began to cry.

I said, "It's okay, I don't blame you, and I'm not holding any ill will toward your stepson. I only wish him Jesus." She then threw her arms around my waist (she only came up to right below my chest) and gave me a very long hug. It was an unforgettable, precious moment.

Friday morning, she didn't return to hear the jury's verdict. Dwayne Ricardo Smith was found guilty of murder in the first-degree. The judge immediately sentenced him to life in prison without the possibility of parole. Court was adjourned. That whole week I asked myself the question, "What's a guy like me doing in a place like this?"

I thanked Erin, the attorney. She signed a form for me to take to a warehouse where evidence is stored to receive what remaining cash was left that had been stolen from Kalvin. Out of approximately $10,000 there was only about $900 left. I used it to partially reimburse myself for Kalvin's cremation cost.

By the way, it was a poignant moment when I left the funeral home with Kalvin's ashes. I didn't expect the box to be so heavy. I thought, "Here I am carrying my big brother who once carried me." I later spread his ashes in the surf on a beach near Wilmington, North Carolina.

A few years after the trial, I wrote a letter to Dwayne Ricardo Smith, who was in the Florida State Prison. All his appeals had been denied. I told him that I'd forgiven him for what he did, and that I wanted him to come to know Jesus and be saved. I wrote out a sinner's prayer for him to pray if he wanted.

He finally wrote back a year later. I'd hoped that my letter might have helped him to turn his life over to Jesus. Instead, his response was filled with vile hatred and accusations of me being a pedophile and another one of those "corrupt priests." He said he didn't need my prayers and that I should pray for myself.

But this story is not over yet! I choose to believe that nobody is too far beyond the amazing grace of Jesus. After all, Jesus reached my brother Kalvin and Jesus reached me. I will continue to ask God to do whatever it takes to reach Dwayne with His great salvation.

As the angel Gabriel said to Mary when he announced that she was chosen to bring forth God's Son...

"...For with God nothing will be impossible."

Luke 1:37 NKJV

Chapter 35

The Vote

Calvary Assembly, where I was still serving, began to greatly decrease in attendance. Many members left when the previous pastor started a new church in town. Others left for various reasons, resulting in a steep decline in finances. The elders of the church consulted with a retired businessman who recommended that the staff needed to be drastically reduced. The church was on a large campus, which included a 5,500-seat auditorium. So, there was a lot of infrastructure to be maintained. The staff cuts came in waves, causing great stress and fear amongst everyone affected. The economy in general was in bad shape, which made the fear of losing a job even more intense. No one was considered non-expendable, it seemed. In October of 2009, my name was added to the list of those who would be let go. It seemed to me, when all the job cuts started, that it was a faithless, strictly business, worldly approach to what was really a spiritual problem.

I met with Pastor George Cope and one of the elders and was notified that I was being let go. They prayed for me and generously offered to pay me through the end of the year, for which I was very grateful. Margie worked at the church as well, in the accounting department, but she was retained.

A few months passed, during which time I sent out resumes and did online searches for a new position. I began to sense that the Lord wanted me to shift into being a senior or lead pastor, so that was the kind of position I began looking for. There were no responses and the faith in my heart began to slowly drain.

I have gone through a few seasons in my life where there didn't seem to be any hope of ministry opportunity on the horizon. During one of those inactive seasons, I turned to Margie and said, "I feel like God has put me on a shelf." A few minutes later, the phone rang, and it was my little buddy Mark Shiver on the line. He said, "I felt strongly that God wanted me to call you and tell you something... He says, *'You are not on the shelf; you are in His lap.'*"

Another time during the four to five months after I was laid off at Calvary Assembly, I attended a special prophetic service at Grace Church. The speaker was Pastor Brady Boyd of New Life Church in Colorado Springs, and during his message he pointed me out. We'd never met before. He asked me my name, then said, *"Jeff, the Lord says to you, 'Harbor time is not wasted time.' During this season, God is loading you up with necessary supplies that you will need to draw from after He launches you out into your next assignment."*

I remember driving one day around the Sanford, Florida area, praying about our situation. It was one of those pitiful, "woe is me", kind of prayers. At one point in the prayer I said, "I'm sorry, Lord, for thinking more highly of myself than I ought. Besides, who do I think I am, thinking that I have what it takes to be a senior pastor?"

Right then, the Lord crashed my pity-party, interrupting my prayer with a strong rebuke. It was as strong as any time I've ever sensed Him speaking to me. He said, *"That's false humility! Stop it now!"*

I said, "Lord, I was only trying to be humble."

He answered, *"True humility does not grovel and whine about what you can't do. True humility agrees with My Word. True humility says, 'I can do all things through Christ who strengthens me!'"*

Wow! I was stunned by the Lord's rebuke, but at the same time, I sensed His great love. God IS love, so even His rebukes and corrections for His children are encased in His unchanging love. I thanked Him, repented, and moved forward with a new perspective.

A few weeks later I received a phone call from the North Carolina District Office of the Assemblies of God. The person said that Dr. Charles Kelly was going to be in Lakeland, Florida that week and he would like to meet with me. Dr. Kelly was the district superintendent over all the Assemblies of God churches in North Carolina.

I drove to Lakeland, which was about an hour from where I lived. I met with Dr. Kelly at a quaint old hotel. As we sat in the lobby, he told me there was a church in Wilmington, North Carolina, that the district was getting ready to close. It had become very small (about 35 people), and the current pastor was too ill to continue and had recently resigned. He offered for me to "try-out" for the church. He said that I would be installed for one year. At the end of that year, the church would hold a business meeting and vote on whether to retain me as their pastor or to release me. I accepted the offer, and we began to make plans to sell our townhouse and move to Wilmington, which was Margie's hometown.

A kind, very soft-spoken man named Jim Bean called me. He was the head of the search committee for the church. We set up a time for me to come to meet with them and to preach for the service. The date was set, we drove up to Wilmington, and stayed with Margie's grandmother. I preached on Sunday morning and then again on Sunday evening, plus I did some music. The church held a vote, and I was elected to be their pastor. Our move to Wilmington coincided with Grace enlisting in the US Navy. We said goodbye to her and hello to a new chapter in our circuitous journey.

My first service as pastor of Wilmington First Assembly of God (WFA) was March 14, 2010. Everyone was super excited and very welcoming to Margie and me. I settled into a rhythm of studying and preparing sermons, meeting with church members, meeting with the church's advisory board, and updating logos, letterhead, signage, etc.

The church was not current on their monthly missions' support. I suggested that we narrow the list down to four or five missionaries/ministries, then take 10% off the top of every offering and set it aside for missions and guest ministers only. I also included supporting the retired previous pastor on a monthly basis.

The first problems I encountered were dealing with the praise and worship team. The team consisted of a decent drummer, an enthusiastic bass player who often didn't show up, an elderly lady playing violin, a young kid playing electric guitar, a man who sang and ran sound, and a lady who led the worship. I'm sorry to say that it sounded embarrassingly bad. I thought, *There is no way that this church will grow with worship being this terrible.* I decided to step in, play guitar, and lead them to help it sound somewhat decent. They were not used to receiving instruction and began to recoil at my leadership. The previous pastor pretty much let them do whatever they wanted, and now the new guy stepped in and started messin' up a good thing.

I began to see different praise team members and some of their friends and family members huddling in corners and hallways whispering. If Margie or I walked by, they got very quiet and looked in different directions. It was pretty obvious.

Since 1999, having received a better understanding of God's grace and the finished work of Jesus on the cross, everything I preached and taught went through the filter of God's grace. One of the praise team members started challenging me about my teaching. Several of them starting having meetings with the previous pastor and would play him CDs of my messages. They came back and reported to others and to me that the previous pastor said my teaching was false.

I felt that this was a serious ethical breach of pastoral protocol. I believe that he should have never entertained their questions and accusations. If he had a concern or question, he should have come to me personally. It is not good for a former pastor to speak against the one who succeeded him. I don't know if it was the flattery of his former congregants coming to him as their spiritual leader, or for some other reason. However, what he did essentially split an already struggling church.

Margie and I carried on, trying to love, shepherd, and lead the church, but the year anniversary of my pastoring was quickly arriving. Prior to the annual business meeting, where I would be voted on to remain or be removed, a few young men that rarely attended sent a letter to Dr. Charles Kelly accusing me of false teaching. Dr. Kelly called me and asked me about it. I sent him a digital copy of the manuscript of every message I had taught since arriving.

The meeting Sunday arrived and the service was pretty tense. The young men who had accused me of false teaching were there for the service, sitting on the front row. I led worship with the praise band and Dr. Kelly preached the message. The service ended and after a ten-minute break the business meeting convened. My spiritual father, Robert Spradley, had driven down from Virginia to be with me that morning and show his support.

Dr. Kelly came up to the platform to conduct the vote. I had to receive a 2/3 majority to be retained as pastor. The ballots were passed out then collected. The count did not take long. Dr. Kelly announced the results. I failed to win a 2/3 majority by one vote.

There was a very awkward silence in that sanctuary. I was asked to come up to say some parting words. I walked up to the front and looked at the congregation and thanked them for allowing me to be their pastor for the past year. I said that I had been stretched and had grown a lot during that time. I ended by saying that I wished them God's best and His blessings.

Some in the church were openly crying. Jim Bean, who had originally contacted me to come and who had been one of my biggest supporters, stood up, took out his large ring of church keys, and threw them on a pew next to one of the other advisory board members who had voted against me. Then he and his wife, Ann, walked out. Jim had been one of the most faithful church leaders and biggest givers for over 30 years.

Dr. Kelly said that the congregation would hear from him shortly regarding the next steps that would be taken. He dismissed the meeting in prayer. He then invited Robert, Margie, and me, out to lunch at Long Horn Steakhouse. We were also joined by Jim and Ann Bean, who had decided to eat there not knowing that we would be there too.

I don't remember much about the conversation over lunch. A lot of it was between Dr. Kelly, Robert, and Jim. I was still reeling from what had just happened, and focused on my steak... (I really like a good ribeye).

Before we left, Dr. Kelly asked me what I was going to do. I said that I'd be driving down to Orlando by myself for a week to rest and pray. It had been so stressful leading up to the vote that we'd decided I would do that either way the vote went. He then said something unexpected. He said, "Jeff, if you don't feel that God is finished with you here, please let me know by Friday." I told him I would. He gave me his personal cell number, and we all shook hands, hugged, and went our separate ways.

The drive to Orlando was another one of those mostly silent drives. My mind kept playing the events that had taken place, over and over again. Were there some things that I could have handled differently to have avoided this humiliating defeat? I searched my heart and honestly, I could not think of any one thing that I would have done differently, except trusting some who said they were with me, but really weren't.

I spent the week driving around, going to some of my favorite places, and met with a few friends. The time there flew by quickly and now it was time to head back. It was Friday morning and I had to decide what to tell Dr. Kelly. I came to the realization that I could not picture me doing anything else besides pastoring this church.

I called him back and gave him my answer. He said, "Okay, I will notify the church that there will be another business meeting this coming Wednesday. I would like for you and Margie to be there." I didn't know what he had in mind, but we made sure that we were there.

We arrived that evening and slipped into my office without being seen. The turnout was pretty big for that small congregation. As Dr. Kelly started the meeting, Margie and I walked into the back of the sanctuary and sat down. The young man who played drums on the praise team, whom I had spent a lot of time with, looked back at us, shocked that we were there. He then mouthed the words, "I'm sorry."

Dr. Kelly began to talk about the church's dysfunctional 60-year history. He reminded them of how they mistreated other pastors who had served there before. He said, "Your pastors have not been your problem. Your problem is YOU!" Then he addressed the accusations of me giving false teaching. He said that he had reviewed all my messages and even retold some of my jokes. He said, "I do not find anything false in Pastor Stockford's teaching. In fact, you have been very blessed to have someone to teach you like this." Somewhere in there he mentioned that they would have a hard time finding another pastor who was willing to come and work for the small amount they were paying me. (So, there's that...)

JEFFERY L. STOCKFORD 173

He then announced that he was placing the church under "District Supervision," which meant the District Office would make any future decisions and was essentially dissolving the church board. He said, "I am reinstating Pastor Stockford as your pastor indefinitely. So now you need to get behind him and move forward in unity!"

He invited everyone up to the front to pray. Most who had cast their vote to have me removed walked out and never returned. Eventually all of them left. There were only about 20 or so members who remained, but we chose to move forward in unity, rowing in the same direction (mostly).

I have told you all this so that you may have peace in Me.
Here on earth you will have many trials and sorrows.
But take heart, because I have overcome the world.

John 16:33 NLT

Chapter 36

Hand Frozen to the Sword

Wilmington First Assembly moved forward for a while in relative peace and unity. We began to slowly grow in attendance. I continued to lead worship on Sunday mornings, then I would set my guitar down and step to the podium to teach the message. Once a quarter we had a pot-luck lunch after the service. On Wednesday nights I taught through the books of the Bible verse by verse. It had a much smaller attendance, but it was my favorite meeting of the week.

My vision for Wilmington First Assembly was for each person to understand the glorious, wonderful New Covenant, and to experience all the benefits Christ purchased for us on the cross. Another priority was that the dysfunction and division that had plagued the church over its 60-year history would cease and that we would be known as a place of genuine love and grace.

We eventually assembled a new advisory board to handle the week-to-week decisions. Some of these board members were later recognized as elders, who not only handled administrative issues but spiritual ones as well.

One of the challenges we had was that the sanctuary could seat about 400 people. Most Sundays we were averaging about 35 in attendance. Visitors would often come and look around at all the empty pews and conclude that there must be some kind of problem with this church. Many never came back. Being so small, with a mostly older congregation, we were not able to offer a full array of ministries such as youth ministry and our volunteer pool was not very deep.

One of the most difficult aspects of pastoring is dealing with people who have an agenda other than the one the Lord has given you. I will relate a few of the challenges I had with some church members that could have potentially destroyed the church. The names have been changed, out of respect for their privacy.

One of the members was Jean, an older widowed lady who was very spunky and full of energy. She had a love for children, and she became the leader of our children's ministry. When we first came, she was one of the most encouraging and supportive people in the church. We had her in our home often, and she volunteered all the time for various projects. At one point I remember saying that it would be a dream if God would send us a whole church full of people like Jean. That dream turned into a nightmare down the road.

God also sent us a young couple, Craig and his wife Mary. They had a young son (who adored Margie), plus a kind mother-in-law. They became very active in the church and were greatly loved by all. However, it didn't last.

Another family I will mention, a young couple named Bob and Karen, with their three kids, came to us with a bad case of "church abuse." Bob and I became very close. We had great conversations and attended a wonderful Grace Conference together, held at Grace Church in Orlando, Florida. He loved his newfound freedom from legalism he discovered through our ministry. He became one of my right-hand men and even did some teaching from time to time. We appointed him the volunteer position of assistant pastor.

Jean, who oversaw our children's ministry, also wanted the church to hold bazaars, (which is "Yankee" for church yard sales) as church fundraisers. She worked tirelessly to collect items to sell, organized the pricing, set things out on tables, and organized the sale of hotdogs and drinks. My mother-in-law, who was not really interested in attending church, loved coming and volunteering to help as a cashier. The bazaars were well attended events, but didn't really net the church much money, though every little bit helped.

We had a couple of these bazaars under our belt, and after one had come to an end, the volunteers were all gathered in a back room, counting the proceeds and getting ready to call it a day. Jean had on one of those aprons with big pockets. I saw her pull out a big wad of cash that she had collected. Jokingly I said, "Jean, what are you going to do with all that money?" Of course, I knew she would never do anything dishonest, and I assumed she knew I was only kidding since we joked together all the time.

Nothing else was said, and Margie and I left to go on a vacation. We came back a few days later, and heard from someone in the church, that Jean was highly offended at what I had said to her about the wad of cash. Immediately, Margie and I went over to her house to try to set the record straight. Jean greeted us at the door with an unusually cold demeanor. For about two hours we sat with her, in her living room, imploring her to believe my comment was simply a lighthearted jest. I profusely apologized, but no matter how much I tried, she refused to believe me. Before we parted, she threatened that if she left the church, she'd take half of the people with her. I began to realize that placing her in a leadership position was a mistake.

She continued to lead the children's ministry and I was informed that Jean had treated three young brothers unkindly. I met with Jean and told her that it was my desire that every child be treated with love, and that each week, every child would hear that Jesus loved them before they went home. I met with the young parents, who were upset about their sons' treatment, and did my best to smooth things over. Unfortunately, Jean ignored what I said, and continued to treat the three boys unfairly. The family decided to leave the church because of it. I also found out that Jean had gone around the church to various people telling them that I didn't want her to teach children the Word of God, I didn't want them to pray, and that I only wanted the children to play games and eat snacks. Jean even said this to Margie... of all people!

I called an emergency meeting of the elders and we met with her. I confronted her again in their presence. I tried to do it in a loving, respectful way, but she was very resistant. I told her that she could no longer serve in church leadership and that she would have to take an extended break from the children's ministry. She acted very strange, and looking back, I believe that she was under the influence of a demonic spirit.

She left the church and as one pastor said to me, "They never leave alone." She "soured" a number of people in the church, and they left with her or shortly after. Even after she was gone, she continued to reach out to some church members and spread poisonous lies.

Craig, whom I mentioned earlier, was a kind, friendly man and his wife, Mary, was a delightful, fun-loving lady. He came early on Sundays and started playing guitar and singing with me during worship. They were both very supportive, and our two families interacted a lot.

One year, our church hosted an event called, *The God Is Not Angry Grace Conference*. Craig and Mary and several others were on the planning committee. We brought in three wonderful grace teachers, James Barron, Noel Cookman, and David Hughes. It turned out to be a really nice event. Some out-of-town guests came to hear the Gospel of Grace boldly proclaimed. We even had t-shirts printed up. Before the conference was over, we started talking about what we wanted to do for the next one.

We started putting plans in motion for the next conference. As the day was approaching, Mary started getting a bit bossy and wanted to push me out of planning and participating in the conference altogether. Then the main speaker, whom we had scheduled, called me to cancel. I spoke with the other speaker, and he said he had some other obligations and also wanted to change the date, but he would honor his commitment if that wasn't possible. Throughout these conversations about the conference, I began to sense that we were trying to force something to happen that maybe God wasn't leading us to do.

I've learned that just because something goes well doesn't necessarily mean it should be repeated. So, I made the decision to cancel the conference for the time being.

When I shared this news with the planning committee, it did not go over well. I received a scathing Facebook message from Mary, questioning my character and fitness to be the pastor, and stating that I was the reason the church was so small and struggling. She and her family left, without speaking a word to me or responding to any of my attempts to contact them to resolve things. That was another huge blow.

The assistant pastor whom I had become very close to, "Bob," had also been poisoned by both Jean and Mary, before and after they left. He was torn between what they were saying about me and his loyalty to me. I could tell he began to pull back from our relationship, and his wife stopped coming to church altogether. One Saturday I met with him to address some things that needed attention in his life, especially being the assistant pastor of the church. He acknowledged the issues and began to weep. I tried to be gentle and kind, but I said he needed to decide whether he was all in or was pulling out. He chose to pull out and leave the church.

This may have been the hardest blow I'd received as a pastor. Looking back, I remember that is exactly how I responded to Robert Spradley's ultimatum after we moved to Raleigh. I chose to pull out as well. I have always regretted that decision.

JEFFERY L. STOCKFORD   179

Now I was beginning to understand how difficult it is to lead a congregation. The rejection and weight a pastor carries on his heart is sometimes unbearable. Only then could I fully appreciate what I had put some of the pastors that I had served under through. I know you can't live your life with regrets, always looking back. However, it made me wish I could go back and do some things over. I may have still ended up at all the different places God has taken me, but like it's said in the prayer of Jabez, *"I wouldn't cause pain."* I am determined with God's help to be a consistent source of blessing to my pastor now.

A couple of times in the 11 years as pastor at Wilmington First Assembly, a young pastor would come to Wilmington to plant a new church within the Assemblies of God. I was subtly pressured to step aside by someone in the headquarters office. I guess it was because they thought with the church being so small, it would be a better use of resources to merge our church into a newer one. I was always willing to do what the district required me to do, because I considered myself as being under their authority. They weren't making me step aside, they hoped I would do it voluntarily. There were many times I would have gladly said, "Here take it, you can have it!" But every time I prayed about it I would begin to see the faces of my little flock. Some of them had special needs. Some of them needed extra attention on Sundays or during the week. Would another pastor come in and take the time to get to know and care for these precious "sheep"? I felt as if I would be abandoning them. So, I dug my heels in and determined to stay until God released me.

In the time I was there, the church went through a lot! A terrible split, one crisis after another, and don't forget about COVID-19. Through it all, we stuck with what we believed to be our assignment from God. There were times Margie and I desperately wished that God would reassign us elsewhere, but we knew He wanted us to remain faithful.

I could write an entire book about the experiences that took place in that little church in Wilmington. But I wanted to convey a few of the major events that shook us and propelled us to trust in our faithful God all the more.

I have forgiven the people who caused such trouble in our lives and the church. Even as I write about these struggles, there is no anger or bitterness in my heart. I have come to understand that we are all at different places in our spiritual development. As you have read already, many of the pastors I served with had to extend much grace to me. I choose to do the same for them.

One of the three of David's Mighty Men was defending a piece of land, and his fellow soldiers deserted him. He stood his ground and prevailed. I have learned that there is great value in standing your ground in ministry. Sometimes it is so tempting to quit and live to fight another day.

I recently heard a retired professional boxer talking about another boxer who had given up after a knock-down. Instead of jumping back to his feet, he stayed on one knee and didn't rise up before the 10-count. The reality was that this boxer had done the same thing a few years earlier in another high stakes fight. This retired boxer made the comment, "The first time you give up and quit will be the hardest. Every time after that, it gets easier and easier."

...Eleazar stood his ground and struck down the Philistines till his hand grew tired and froze to the sword. The LORD brought about a great victory that day...

2 Samuel 23:10 NIV

Chapter 37

A Blunt and Bent Nail

COVID-19 happened, along with the rules and face-mask mandates, then came the church shutdowns. Out of necessity, we started doing our services on Facebook Live, which turned out to be a pleasant surprise. We had a few hundred watching on some weeks. With the church being so small, we were able to come under some of the number restrictions and legally began meeting publicly again. We decided to come out of the big, mostly empty sanctuary, and instead gather in the fellowship hall, which was much more intimate. We had a wonderful time in this setting, and I wished that we had made the move sooner. Margie and I both think this was the best season of pastoral ministry we had experienced in all the time we had served there. It became less of a formal service and more of a family gathering.

In the previous chapter, I wrote of some families and individuals who made pastoring difficult. But that isn't the complete picture. They were the exception and not the rule. There were a number of wonderful, faithful, loving members of our church. They prayed for us and encouraged us throughout our journey. I don't know if I could have lasted without their support and friendship. I am afraid that if I mentioned them by name, I might forget someone, and they would be hurt. So, if you were one of those who hung in there with us, you are who I am referring to.

I didn't mention that along with coming to Wilmington to pastor WFA, Margie's parents and grandmother were aging and had come into stages of life where they needed help. Our move there coincided with their need for transportation. Margie's father had to be committed to a memory care facility because of dementia. For about eight years, I drove Barbara, Margie's mom, to visit him every Monday and Friday and then took her to buy groceries. Margie's grandmother also had to go into a nursing home, though her mind was still sharp as a tack. She had reached the age of 103 and could no longer care for herself. Eventually even Barbara had to go into an assisted living facility because it became unsafe for her to live alone, as she had several bad "face-planting" falls. None of them wanted to live with us, that was made clear! Over our time there, all three passed away.

Margie had stopped working in the financial field to care for her mother the last few years before Barbara went into assisted living. She handled all the business and estate matters. God works on more than one level at a time, as only He can orchestrate.

One Saturday after preparing the fellowship hall for the service on Sunday, I was walking to my car, and as He had done numerous times, God spoke in my spirit, saying, *"Your season of pastoring this church has come to an end."*

Nothing was wrong. Things were going easier in this season than any time before. I wasn't asking God to reassign me. But the word was very clear. I went home and shared that with Margie, who has a very wise and discerning heart. She agreed. I contacted the Assemblies of God District Superintendent, who was now Dr. Rick Ross, to set up an appointment to meet with him in Raleigh. WFA was still under district supervision, as it had been since "the vote." We relayed what we were sensing from the Lord to Dr. Ross, and he was extremely kind and encouraging. He thanked us for being faithful and said his office would be in contact on how to proceed. I also asked him to decide when I should step down, as I didn't want to create another problem for him. He was already dealing with about 15 other churches who were in crisis.

He called me back and said my last service would be May 2, 2021. He then informed me that that day would also be the final service for Wilmington First Assembly. They had decided to close the church and sell the property. The congregation was to be encouraged to attend another Assemblies of God church in Wilmington.

The public announcement was made two weeks prior to the final service. Most were upset and wanted us to stay. However, the decision had been made and was now out of my hands. The final service was well attended. We packed out the fellowship hall. Jim Kelly, my old pal, who now worked for the District Office, came to lead the meeting. My dear friend Pastor Ron Barnard came as well, to invite the congregation to his church. David and Lisa Hughes, who had become and still are some of our dearest friends, drove down from Benson, North Carolina to be with us for that day too.

The service was dismissed and just like that, the most challenging and rewarding season of my life (up to that point) had come to an end.

After the final service, Margie and I went to Florida for a vacation. We also drove out to Dallas, Texas to visit with our dear friends Noel and Gay Cookman. This was an enjoyable time of doing some traveling. We also went to a conference in Nashville, Tennessee hosted by Pastor Kent and Candy Christmas, some of our favorite preachers in the universe. We even stayed in the Opryland Hotel, which had been on my bucket list. It was an enjoyable time without responsibilities and the pressures of ministry.

I sensed that the Lord's instruction to me in this season was to rest. Unfortunately, I squandered much of that time when I should have been at rest, trying to figure out what and where was my next ministry assignment.

During this time, I met a young couple, David and Jillian Freeland, who had moved to Wilmington to plant a church. We met for coffee (I had a milkshake) and we really hit it off. Margie and I had dinner with them one evening in their home. They wanted us to join them and help them plant a new church in the Wilmington area. But I didn't sense a green light from the Lord to commit to doing that.

The former WFA property was put on the market and eventually purchased by Multiply Church, a large church in Concord, North Carolina. Multiply Church wanted to add a campus in Wilmington. My new friends David and Jillian Freeland connected with them, and became the pastors of the new Multiply Church of Wilmington, meeting in what had been our Wilmington First Assembly's old church building.

With the backing of Multiply Church in Concord, they were able to completely renovate the outdated building into a beautiful, modern facility. The grand opening was packed out with excited worshippers and has been growing ever since. It occurred to me that the old church had to die in order for this new church, which is full of life and vibrancy, to be birthed.

I couldn't help but feel like a failure. I spent over eleven years there, trying to bring a dying church back to life, seeing very little success. Now a new church comes into the old facility and it is busting at the seams. I had been dealing with this sense of failure most of the time there at WFA, especially when I attended the North Carolina District ministers' events. There I would see other churches being highlighted and recognized for their growth and accomplishments. I thought, *It's too bad they don't recognize pastors who are struggling to keep the lights on and keep their sanity.* I would usually come home from those events depressed and discouraged.

But something happened that changed my perspective on my time there as pastor of WFA. I met with David Freeland one more time at the Cracker Barrel restaurant. Margie and I were getting ready to move to a different region of the state, for reasons I will share in the next chapter. David said he had something he wanted to give to me.

During breakfast he pulled out of his pocket an old nail that had been taken out of the ceiling during the church's renovation. He said that he wanted to give it to me as a memento of our time there. He said I was a big part of the church's history and one of the reasons that they are enjoying the blessings of God now. I was touched that he would acknowledge me. We finished our meal and conversation and parted.

I sat in my car for a few minutes looking at the six-inch nail. It was kind of bent and the point was blunt, like it had been pounded into a very hard surface. I thought, *That seems fitting.* When I shared it with Margie, she sensed the Holy Spirit saying, *"Son and daughter, I have seen what you have been through. You were hammered into a hard surface for My purpose. Though bent and blunted, you held strong and remained faithful. I want you to know that it was not in vain, and you did not fail. I will reward you."*

I remember some years before as I was taking another step of faith to record my album, "Leaving Familiar," the Lord spoke to me and said, *"Other people's destinies are attached to yours. Your steps of faith and obedience will affect them as well as you."*

And I thank Christ Jesus our Lord who has enabled
me, because He counted me faithful,
putting me into the ministry,

1 Timothy 1:12 NKJV

Chapter 38

A Place I Never Imagined

During this time the Lord opened up doors for me to minister in music and share about what Jesus had done in my life, in various churches. It's always been my favorite thing to do in ministry. God is so kind and gracious to allow me to be involved in something I love, while waiting for what He has for us next. I also recorded and released my sixth album, "A Psalmist's Journal." It was a double CD album. It featured new, never released songs as well as some earlier recorded songs. Kind of a "Best of..." album.

In the fall of 2021, we received a call from our daughter Grace and her husband Carsen with news that they were pregnant. We also learned that Carsen, who was serving in the US Navy, was scheduled to be deployed at sea around the time the baby was due and afterward. Margie and I had been seeking God for what He wanted for us to do in this next season. Now it became pretty clear: we needed to move up near Chesapeake, Virginia, to be close to our daughter and soon-coming grandbaby. We immediately began to search for a house to buy in one of the craziest real estate markets in history.

I hurriedly made about 12 different trips up to Chesapeake and the surrounding areas, as soon as a prospective house came on the market. We put offers on several houses, only to be outbid on all of them. I reached the point of giving up and considering that perhaps it wasn't God's will for us to move almost five hours away.

It came time for Grace to give birth and we were watching our phones, waiting for the call. Carsen was able to get off the ship and be with Grace for the delivery. The call finally came, and our baby princess granddaughter arrived healthy and strong. We made the drive to the hospital and finally got to meet Solveig Shoshana. Solveig (pronounced Sole-vay) is Scandinavian for "sunshine." Shoshana is Hebrew for "lily." Grace was doing well and had come through with flying colors.

We had a wonderful time visiting with them at the hospital, but eventually we had to go back to Wilmington. We would have to make do with texting photos and FaceTime chats.

When Grace went back to work, she enrolled Solveig in a daycare center that had cameras in the infant room. I got the access code and spent many hours watching her. It was hard because she did a lot of crying and kicking her legs. Sometimes I'd see some little kid step on her or drop a toy on her head. I found myself wanting to scream at the screen and jump in my car and drive up there. I eventually had to look away for the sake of my blood pressure and pray for her instead.

Margie went up to stay with Grace and Solveig one week while Carsen was out to sea. She said that she would do some house shopping while up that way. She prayed and she believed that the Lord revealed to her that He would bring her to the right house before she left. During that week, she saw a nice house that seemed to check off most of the boxes. She went there with our realtor and loved the neighborhood and the house. She put in an offer, but it was turned down.

She was getting ready to pack up and come home on Friday. She looked on her real estate app one more time and saw that the house next door had been listed on the market. She met our realtor there and it was even better than the first house, and included a screened in porch, which is something we both really wanted. She made the offer, it was accepted, and we closed the following month!

We made the move in 2023 to our new home in Shawboro, North Carolina, surrounded by corn and barley fields. This was the closest I had ever been to living in the country. Our house was about 15 minutes from the nearest gas station and fast-food joint, and about 35 minutes from our daughter and her family in Chesapeake. The country life takes some getting used to, for a city boy. The most excitement is when the yellow crop-duster swoops over our house.

As of the time of this writing, Margie is the daily babysitter for baby princess, Solveig. I am her trusty helper. I used to be known as Pastor or Reverend Stockford. My new official title is Assistant Nanny, 2nd Class.

Living in a rural community and helping to care for my beautiful granddaughter wasn't on my radar. This is a place I never imagined, and one of the most delightful detours God has placed in my route.

There is one last story I'd like to share before this book is finished, because of its impact on my life. One of the families that I have been closest to are the Cookmans, Noel, Gay, and their two sons, Zack and Andy. I met Noel when he was a youth pastor in Concord, North Carolina. He was leading a ministry called The Potter's House. Noel graciously invited me to come there to minister in music. Through the years, wherever God has used Noel, he would include me in some way. His father was Dr. Charles Cookman, who was the former superintendent of the North Carolina District Assemblies of God, and a dear sweet friend. He was the most Christ-like man I've ever known. Dr. Cookman took a liking to me and allowed me many opportunities to minister throughout the state of North Carolina at various ministry events.

I've never felt so loved and encouraged as when I am able to spend time with any one of the Cookmans. The gift of encouragement, well, they all have it, the sons, Zack and Andy, as much as their parents and grandparents. There's so much I can say about each member of this wonderful family that could fill a whole other book. However, I am going to focus on one event.

Zack Cookman did something for me that I'll never forget. In 1999, Margie and I were vacationing in Orlando, Florida, and ended up in the home of James and Cindy Barron. James was the one who introduced me to the gospel of grace, through the finished work of Christ. It was the most transforming revelation I've experienced since the day I was born again. James was leading a Bible study in his packed living room. He invited me to get my guitar and share some songs. At that meeting, we went into a sweet time of worship and the presence of the Holy Spirit was very powerful! Our friends the Cookmans were there as well.

Afterward, as we were standing around fellowshipping, Zack approached me to say that someday he wanted to capture a live recording of me playing in an intimate worship environment like that. I was touched that God had put that in his heart, but at the time it didn't seem feasible. We went back to Pittsburg after our vacation, and I forgot about what Zack said.

Fast-forward about 15 years. Zack had not forgotten about his desire to capture that experience in a recording. He approached me about it again and I was so touched that he remembered and still wanted to do it. Now, Zack had the wherewithal and contacts to make it happen. He organized the event, invited some friends and provided some food. That night in 2013, a group of friends gathered. Paul Clawson joined me on drums and Robbie Brown played the upright bass and provided the house and recording equipment. We played and sang some of my worship songs. We later released it on a project called "No Place Like Home."

Zack made all of that happen. He did what he said he would do, even more than a decade later. A pastor once made the statement, "The most important word in the English language is 'others.'" Zack embodied this, sharing his many talents and incredible humor to brighten up everybody's lives. He rubbed shoulders with many of the A-listers in Hollywood and won them over with his kindness and hilarious dry wit.

I titled this chapter "A Place I Never Imagined," and that is certainly true of our present place of residence and lifestyle. But there is another place I never imagined I'd be. It was at a church in Raleigh to be part of a memorial service. Zack had been in the hospital bravely fighting leukemia and on February 24, 2023, he finished his race and went to be with Jesus. Even while in the hospital he was extending God's love and grace to "others," all the way to the end.

The memorial service was incredible with inspiring music, amazing speakers, and wonderful memories that were shared of Zack's short but impactful life. The part that touched me to the core was when Noel, Zack's father, stepped up at the end and spoke some parting words. They were simple, yet some of the most powerfully profound words ever spoken. I will try to paraphrase what he said:

"People have asked me what I am going to do now that Zack has passed. I'll tell you what I'm not going to do. I'm not going to ask God why. Because I don't think He will tell me. I'm also afraid that if He did, it might have something to do with me.

Here is what I'm going to do. I am going to keep putting one foot in front of the other and keep moving forward. I'm going to do that not knowing the answers. Because God is still good, and I need Him every hour."

This is how we all get through the many challenges, tragedies, setbacks, abuses, failures, and sorrows that come with living in a fallen world. We don't focus on the "whys" but we focus on the "Who," and that is Jesus, the One who already ran the race before us and won the victor's crown. What is so amazing to me is that He placed His crown on our head and declared us the champion.

Whoever you are, keep putting one foot in front of the other. Don't quit. God is with you no matter what! God is with you even if He chooses to take you "another way" than you expected.

I testify to you today that my Heavenly Tour Guide has been with me every step of the way and has proven His love and faithfulness over and over again. He has done this even through the times when I felt I was the most unlovable and unfaithful. I have no doubt whatsoever that Jesus will lovingly and skillfully guide you all the way until you reach your destination. Trust Him, follow His lead, and give yourself to Him wholeheartedly.

Though this book has ended, there are still chapters to be written. I turned 62 today, but I believe my best days are ahead! As He did at the wedding in Cana with changing the water into wine, I believe Jesus has saved the best for last! I'm grateful He has taken me another way.

Finally, brethren, farewell. Become complete. Be of good comfort, be of one mind, live in peace; and the God of love and peace will be with you... The grace of the Lord Jesus Christ, and the love of God, and the communion of the Holy Spirit be with you all. Amen

2 Corinthians 13:11,14 NKJV